GOD'S LIVING WORD

MATTHEW

A Catholic Guide
for Personal Study and
Faith Sharing

GOD'S LIVING WORD

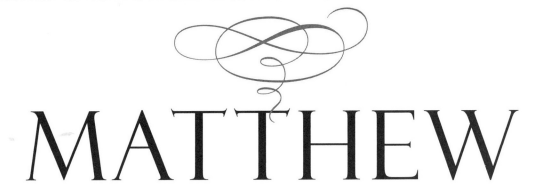

MATTHEW

A Catholic Guide for Personal Study and Faith Sharing

Edited by Steven Roe

theWORD among us® press

The Word Among Us Press
9639 Doctor Perry Road
Ijamsville, Maryland 21754
www.wordamongus.org

ISBN: 978-1-59325-092-8

12 11 10 09 08   1 2 3 4 5

Nihil Obstat: Dr. Robert D. Miller II, SFO
               February 12, 2008
Imprimatur: +Most Reverend W. Francis Malooly, DD, VG
               Auxiliary Bishop of Baltimore
               February 12, 2008

Cover and text design: David Crosson

Cover Image:
Giotto di Bondone (1266-1336)
Flight into Egypt.
Location: Scrovegni Chapel, Padua, Italy
Photo credit: Alinari/Art Resource, NY

Library of Congress Control Number: 2007938465

CONTENTS

Preface: Welcome to the New Testament, God's Living Word   6

Customizing Your Visit—Four Bible Study Plans   8

How To's for Individuals and Groups   11

An Introduction to Matthew's Gospel   18
      By Fr. Joseph A. Mindling, OFM Cap

Walking with Jesus in the Holy Land   22
      By Fr. Joseph A. Mindling, OFM Cap

Scripture Meditations   25

The Passion of Christ (26:1–27:66)   131
      By Gregory Roa

Appendix 1: Index of Meditations   138

Appendix 2: Reading through the Liturgical Year   141

PREFACE

WELCOME TO THE NEW TESTAMENT,

GOD'S LIVING WORD

Have you ever gone on vacation to a major theme park without the help of a detailed visitors' guide? No doubt you planned your trip full of anticipation and excitement about the thrills you would experience and the sights you would see. And yet you may have been frustrated when the vacation was over, because you didn't see as much of the park as you'd hoped to. If only you had known ahead of time which attractions are a "must," and what order seasoned park-goers recommend seeing them in!

Reading and applying God's word in the Bible can be a lot like visiting that much-anticipated theme park. You can open the Scriptures filled with excitement about learning what God has to say to you and what it means for your life. And yet you can sometimes wind up just as frustrated that you didn't fully understand his message. If only there were visitors' guides to help you get the most out of reading the Bible!

It was to provide you with a set of "visitors' guides to the Scriptures" that the books in this series were developed. Designed for both parish faith-sharing groups and individual use, each guide takes you, from beginning to end, through a particular book or set of books in the New Testament, pointing out the highlights along the way and encouraging you to make the most of your experience of Scripture. The Scripture texts are divided into short passages, and each citation is followed by a meditation and a set of three reflection questions.

Theme parks often have so much to offer that fully experiencing them in one visit isn't always feasible. And so attractions are often grouped into "packages" that are designed for different age groups or interests and that can be completed in a particular amount of time. Similarly, most of the books of the New Testament contain more riches than could adequately be explored in a single Bible study. For that reason, each book in the series offers four different "packages" that can be covered in eight-week periods. Each package or plan explores a particular theme by combining eight sets of meditations and reflection questions from among the dozens provided in the book. You can choose the package or packages that most appeal to you or your group, or feel free to use them as suggestions for creating your own unique Bible study. In case you would like to coordinate your choice of readings with the Mass, we also list the Sunday readings for each of the three cycles of the liturgical year (see Appendix 2, pp. 141–47).

To help you get the most out of the particular group of readings you choose to study, we provide "how-to's" for using the meditations and questions in a faith-sharing group as well as for personal reflection. For groups, we have designed each session to be completed in sixty to ninety minutes, but you can easily adjust them to meet your particular needs. We also offer practical pointers for forming a faith-sharing group and dealing with group dynamics. A coordinators' guide is available for parishes and others who would like more detailed information about starting and facilitating their own programs.

Finally, because people come to the Bible with different backgrounds, we include general overviews of each book of the New Testament written by respected Scripture scholars, as well as articles that explore the culture and issues of the time. The insights in these materials will enrich your experience of the readings and provide interesting points of departure for reflection or discussion.

Whether studying the meditations in this book by yourself or with a group, prepare yourself for a life-changing adventure. Reflecting on Scripture transforms us—personally and communally—because it is the *living* word of God. We cannot be the same after we have spent time with God's word, because it comes to dwell in us. And we are meant to take that word out to others—through our words, actions, and attitudes—and make a difference with it.

Our sincere hope and prayer is that the guidelines presented here assist you in embracing God's word with your whole heart, mind, and soul—then, with passion and love, unleash it to the world.

So welcome to the New Testament! May you have a rewarding visit to the Gospel of Matthew and return to the Scriptures again and again.

The Word Among Us Press

CUSTOMIZING YOUR VISIT

Four Bible Study Plans

Do you have a faith-sharing group that would like to explore the ways Matthew reveals that Jesus is the Messiah? Or do you have a group that would prefer an overview or introduction to the Gospel of Matthew? Whatever the background or interests of your particular group of people, you can combine the many meditations in this guide to create a study of Matthew that they will all find rewarding.

We have suggested four Bible study "packages" below, designed to provide different approaches to the Gospel of Matthew. Each package explores a particular theme in Matthew or looks at Matthew from a particular perspective, and includes eight sessions designed to be studied one per week over an eight-week period. (Experienced Bible study leaders consider eight weeks to be the ideal duration for first-time faith-sharing groups as well as for longer-standing groups.) You should feel free to blend programs and shorten or lengthen them to meet your individual needs. You can also use the programs as examples to combine readings in other ways to create a program that matches the specific interests of your group. To make it easy to coordinate them with the Sunday Mass readings or seasons, we have provided a list of readings for the three cycles of the liturgical year (see Appendix 2, pp. 141–47).

You will also find the programs below well suited for personal study—whether you are currently in a Bible study group or not. Or you could choose to proceed through the meditations from beginning to end and cover the entire Gospel of Matthew at your own pace.

Plan 1: An Overview of Matthew's Gospel—Eight Key Passages

You may want to begin with an eight-week overview of Matthew's gospel. The list below divides the gospel into eight major sections. To ensure that you study the full range of passages, we recommend choosing one or two passages from each section:

Week 1: The Birth of Jesus and the Beginning of his Ministry (1:1–4:11), pp. 25–31
Week 2: The Sermon on the Mount and the Miracles in Galilee (4:12–9:38), pp. 32–60
Week 3: Jesus' Messages to Missionaries (10:1–12:50), pp. 61–77
Week 4: The Parables and Acknowledging Jesus as the Messiah (13:1–17:27), pp. 78–99
Week 5: Jesus' Teachings on Community and Forgiveness (18:1–20:34), pp. 100–110
Week 6: Jesus' Teachings on the End Times and Persecution (21:1–25:46), pp. 111–30
Week 7: Jesus' Passion and Death (26:1–27:66), pp. 131–35 (The passion narrative is covered in one session but is accompanied by eight questions instead of three. Your group might want to schedule additional time or add an extra session in order to cover all the points.)
Week 8: Jesus' Resurrection (28:1-20), pp. 136–37

An overview based on the above plan might look like this:

Week 1: The Birth of the Messiah: Obedient and Dedicated Faith (1:18-25), p. 26
Week 2: Sermon on the Mount: Fulfilling the Law and the Prophets (5:17-19), p. 35
Week 3: Message to Missionaries: Commissioning the Apostles to Preach (10:1-7), p. 61
Week 4: A Parable: Rooted in Good Soil (13:1-9), p. 78
Week 5: Jesus' Teaching: The Privilege of Serving Christ (20:1-16), p. 108
Week 6: On the End Times: God's Blessing on the Sheepfold (25:31-46), p. 130
Week 7: Jesus' Passion: The Passion of Christ (26:1–27:66), pp. 131–35
Week 8: Jesus' Resurrection: Kingdom Courage Overcomes Fear and Death (28:1-15), p. 136

Plan 2: Jesus' Ethical Teachings—The Sermon on the Mount (Matthew 5–7)

The second Bible study plan covers Jesus' rich and rewarding ethical teachings, which he delivered in his Sermon on the Mount (Matthew 5–7):

Week 1: Abundant Blessings (5:1-12), p. 33
Week 2: Salt of the Earth, Light of the World (5:13-16), p. 34
Week 3: Forgiveness Rather Than Retaliation (5:38-42), p. 39
Week 4: Love for Enemies (5:43-48), p. 40
Week 5: The Motives of Charity (6:1-6, 16-18), p. 41
Week 6: Serve God and Worry Not (6:24-34), p. 44
Week 7: Prayer According to God's Will (7:7-12), p. 46
Week 8: Acting Upon the Father's Will (7:21-29), p. 48

Plan 3: Jesus the Messiah Inaugurates the Kingdom of Heaven

The third Bible study plan looks at Matthew's slow and steady unveiling of Jesus' true identity as the Messiah who comes to inaugurate the kingdom of heaven:

Week 1: Gifts for the King (2:1-12), p. 27
Week 2: The Servant's Baptism (3:13-17), p. 30
Week 3: The Christian Mission (4:12-25), p. 32
Week 4: Recognizing the Messiah (12:14-21), p. 73
Week 5: The Christ, the Son of the Living God (16:13-20), p. 94
Week 6: Transformed into the Image of Christ (17:1-9), p. 96
Week 7: Jesus' Humble Entry into Jerusalem (21:1-11), p. 111
Week 8: The Coming Day of the Lord (24:1-35), p. 125

Plan 4: Responding to Jesus' Call to Discipleship

The fourth Bible study plan includes passages that call you to strengthen and deepen your faith in Jesus:

Week 1: Repentance and the Spirit's Guidance (3:1-12), p. 29
Week 2: Reconciling with One Another (5:20-26), p. 36
Week 3: The Primacy of Mercy (12:1-8), p. 71
Week 4: Yielding Plentiful Fruit (13:18-23), p. 80
Week 5: Trusting in the Lord (14:22-36), p. 89
Week 6: Forgiveness from the Heart, Without Limit (18:21-35), p. 103
Week 7: The Readiness of the Wise (25:1-13), p. 128
Week 8: The Great Commission (28:16-20), p. 137

HOW-TO'S FOR INDIVIDUALS AND GROUPS

Maybe you'd like to start a faith-sharing group in your parish, or perhaps you've decided to devote some time to personal reflection on Scripture. Where do you begin? How should you structure your time? How can you use the meditations and questions in this guide? What if you run into problems?

Here we provide answers to those questions and more by offering the collected wisdom of experienced faith-sharing and Bible-study group leaders and retreat masters. We'll get you started, show you how to plan each session, and offer suggestions for ensuring that your individual or group experience is a success.

Individual Reflection

Reading and reflecting on Scripture by yourself is a wonderful way to develop a personal relationship with God—and one that can be just as rewarding as participating in a faith-sharing group. When praying on your own, you can choose to go through the meditations in order or choose one of the "packages" mentioned above (see pp. 8–10). You can even choose meditations that correspond to each Sunday's Mass readings (see Appendix 2, pp. 141–47). When praying on your own, you're free to choose the meditations and the pace that work best for you.

Before you begin your journey, read "An Introduction to Matthew's Gospel" on pp. 18–21 and "Walking with Jesus in the Holy Land" (pp. 22–24). This background material will give you insight into Matthew's style of writing and the context of the events he recounted in his gospel.

When you're ready to start the meditations, choose a time and a place that are free of distractions and that allow you to devote at least thirty minutes to each meditation. To help you develop a fruitful practice of studying and praying with Scripture, we suggest using the following pattern: *gather, listen, respond, go forth*. This echoes the pattern recommended for group faith sharing, described on pp. 12–17.

1. Gather

In the *gather* step, you prepare yourself mentally and physically to hear what God has to say to you in this session. Light a candle as a reminder of God's constant presence within and around you. Then open your Bible to the passage cited in the meditation. Close your eyes, inhale slowly and deeply, and then exhale. As you exhale, let go of any distractions and quiet your heart. Pray for openness to God's word.

2. Listen

The second step is to really *listen* to God's word. Read the Scripture passage slowly—aloud, if possible, so that you hear the sound of each of the words. Notice what word or phrase or sentence resonates within you; underline it in your Bible, or write it down. Read the passage again. Sit quietly with the word of God for a few moments.

3. Respond

Now that you have listened to the word of God, allow yourself to *respond* to it. Note any insights, questions, or challenges that enter your reflections; you might write these thoughts in a journal. Then read the short meditation. Ponder the reflection questions, and write your responses in a journal, if you wish. Challenge yourself to be completely honest, and open yourself to God's influence.

4. Go Forth

Now it's time to prepare yourself to *go forth* and apply what you have experienced in this session. Ask yourself, "How will I be different for learning about and reflecting on this passage of God's word? What will I take from this time of prayer into my day today?" Bring your prayers of petition and thanksgiving to God. Pray a closing blessing, such as the following:

"Loving God, bless me and hold me today. Let your word come alive in my heart, my words, and my actions. May I go in peace to love and serve you and those you place in my life this day. Amen."

Group Faith Sharing

Our prayer and faith are deepened when shared in community. If you wish to gather others to join you in reflecting on the meditations in this book, you might simply extend an invitation to friends and acquaintances, or work with your church to establish a more formal program. We offer general guidelines here for organizing a faith-sharing group and effectively managing group dynamics. More detailed instructions for administering faith-sharing groups can be found in *The Coordinators' Guide for Group Faith Sharing*, available at the Word Among Us Web site, www.wau.org/godslivingword.

Forming the Group

Determine a place and time to meet. Your group may choose to meet weekly, biweekly, or monthly—at a place and time that is convenient for the members. Homes are especially suited to gatherings like this. You might choose to meet at the facilitator's home, or different members of the group could take turns hosting the meetings. You might also decide to meet at a room in your church.

When determining when and how often to meet, here are possible options to consider:
* the seasons of Advent or Lent, summer, or midwinter;
* eight sessions, based on one of the Bible study plans presented on pp. 8–10;
* a long-term basis, studying each of the meditations from the beginning of the book to the end.

The time of day to meet is best determined by the needs of the members. People who work during the day might prefer evening meetings; people who are at home or retired might prefer to meet during the day. If the members have small children, you might ask if your parish could provide babysitting.

Each group gathering typically lasts between sixty and ninety minutes. Time estimates are provided below as guidelines for a ninety-minute meeting; your group can decide to spend more or less time on particular topics according to your needs and interests. We recommend that groups work with just one meditation at each meeting. This allows for a relaxed pace and time to simply enjoy one another's company.

Select a facilitator for the meetings. This could be the same person for all of the sessions, or members of the group could take turns leading the sessions. The facilitator's role includes guiding the members through each activity in the time allotted, keeping the discussion on track, and ensuring that everyone has a chance to participate. The facilitator will also want to select the prayers or music that will be used to open or close the meetings, since these should be coordinated with the theme of the session.

The facilitator is responsible for the "nuts and bolts" of the meetings, such as ordering materials and collecting fees, informing members of changes in times or locations, and determining who will host the meetings or provide drinks and snacks.

If your faith-sharing group is part of a church-sponsored program, your parish coordinator may offer training and formation for the facilitators. Training suggestions and additional information for facilitators are provided in *The Coordinator's Guide for Group Faith Sharing.*

Provide enough materials for everyone. Each member should receive a copy of the Scripture guide so that they can review the material before the meeting. Discussions are always more fruitful when participants have had time to reflect on the material than when they come to it cold.

Each participant should also bring a Bible to the meetings. If you like, you can specify a particular translation. Using the same translation has the advantage that everyone in the group is reading and responding to the same words. Yet, allowing different translations enables people to use their personal Bible, and different wording can serve as points of departure for discussion. If you have a preferred translation and your group is part of a larger parish program, your parish could order Bibles in bulk and make them available for purchase.

Members should also be encouraged to bring a journal or notebook to record their thoughts on the readings and meditations, as well as their responses to the reflection questions.

Encourage regular attendance. Your faith-sharing group will be the most productive if members attend as many sessions as possible. Regular attendance demonstrates commitment to the group, ensures continuity across the sessions, and helps everyone get the most from the faith-sharing experience. If participants have to miss a meeting, they can read the Scripture passage and meditation on their own and reflect on their answers to the questions. (See the section "Individual Reflection" on pp. 11–12.) Then they will be ready to rejoin the group at the next session.

Structuring the Sessions

The same progression/pattern described for individuals—*gather, listen, respond, go forth*—is recommended when you use this guide to journey with a group.

Valuable background information about Matthew's gospel and the culture of the time can be found in the supplementary materials in this guide, "An Introduction to Matthew's Gospel" (pp. 18–21) and "Walking with Jesus in the Holy Land" pp. 22–24). Participants should read these chapters independently before any of the sessions begin. The group can choose to discuss them at either an introductory session or throughout the meetings as they apply to particular topics.

The passion narrative in Matthew's gospel (26:1–27:66) is covered in one session in this guide ("The Passion of Christ," pp. 131–34) and is accompanied by eight questions instead of three. So when you come to this session, your group might want to schedule additional time in order to cover all the points.

1. Gather (20 minutes)
Hospitality

Whatever location you choose for your Bible study, you'll want to create an environment that is conducive to reflection and faith sharing by paying attention to comfortable seating, temperature, and light. Offer beverages and perhaps a simple snack. Provide name tags until group members know each other's names. Warmly welcome the participants as they enter the home or meeting space. Initiate introductions—when the group is new, and as new participants join an established group.

An enjoyable and effective technique for getting acquainted is to have participants interview another member of the group whom they don't already know well and then introduce that person to the group.

Prayer

When you're ready to begin, light a candle to represent God's presence among the group. Then gather everyone with an opening prayer or song to set the tone for the meeting. The facilitator can model the opening for a few meetings and then assign it to different members of the group. You might use one of the following, or select or compose your own prayer related to the topic of the meeting:

■ the Sign of the Cross;

■ a simple invitation to prayer, such as, "Let us remember that we are in the holy presence of God" (from the tradition of St. John Baptist de la Salle);

- a litany, such as the following:

  > **Leader:** Open our ears, Lord.
  > **All:** We thirst for your living Word.
  > **Leader:** Open our minds, Lord.
  > **All:** We thirst for understanding.
  > **Leader:** Open our hearts, Lord.
  > **All:** We thirst for your truth and wisdom.
  > **Leader:** Open our hands, Lord.
  > **All:** We thirst for friendship and generosity in this community.

- a simple song that can be sung together (with or without instrumental accompaniment), such as, "Open My Eyes" by Jesse Manibusan, or "Come and Fill" by the Taizé community (both are available in the hymnal *Gather Comprehensive*, Second Edition, GIA Publications);

- or even, if any of the group members have musical talent, a reflective song relating to the Scripture message that they perform or lead for the group.

Community Sharing

Invite participants to share what is new in their lives—joys, struggles, concerns, dreams, and so on. Consider posing this question: "How have you felt God's presence or absence in your life since the last time we met?"

2. Listen (10 minutes)

Ask someone in the group to read the Scripture passage for the session aloud, and invite the others to follow along in their own Bibles or simply to listen. After allowing a few moments of quiet, reread the passage aloud. You may wish to have a different person read it the second time, because differences in delivery can affect the way the passage is interpreted by listeners. If participants are using different Bibles, you might choose to read the passage from a couple of different translations.

3. Respond (40 minutes)

Invite participants to share whatever spoke to them from the Scripture passage—any insights, challenges, connections to their own experiences, questions, and so on. If you wish, allow a few minutes for quiet reflection or journaling before sharing aloud. Ask someone in the group to read the meditation in the guide aloud, and invite comments on it. Then engage the group in dialogue, using the reflection questions.

4. Go Forth (20 minutes)

Mission

Urge the participants to consider how God's word will live in them as they return to their daily routine: "How is God calling or challenging you personally through the Scripture passage we reflected on?" "How might God be calling this group to reach out to the greater community—local or global?"

Prayer

Quiet the group for a closing prayer. The prayer brings closure to the meeting by inviting the participants to live out God's message in the coming week. Invite any prayers of petition or thanksgiving from the participants. Then lead the group in praying a blessing, such as

"Loving God, bless us and hold us as we leave this place. Let your word come alive in our hearts, our words, and our actions. May we go in peace to love and serve you and those you place in our lives. Amen."

Small-Group Dynamics

Adapting to the dynamics of your particular group will help everyone involved have a positive faith-sharing experience. The group facilitator will work to keep the faith-sharing process flowing smoothly by watching time limits, directing discussions, and creating opportunities for everyone to have a chance to express their thoughts. Others in the group can support this effort and ensure rich discussion by participating with respect and openness. Here are some guidelines to keep in mind:

Be aware of time when you're sharing. Time for group sharing is limited, and everyone should feel that they have a chance to contribute to the dialogue. Try to keep your input brief so that you won't monopolize the discussion.

Speak from your heart—take some risks. You may prefer to keep your reflections to yourself. But often what you say aloud can change another person's perspective or offer hope or inspiration by letting them know that they're not alone. So be brave, and speak what's on your mind!

Listen openly. Expect that God will speak to you through other people. Even if the opinions of others seem to be in conflict with your own values, see if there is anything you could learn from their perspective.

Appreciate diversity. A variety of personality types will contribute to lively dialogue. And considering an assortment of viewpoints will broaden the experience of everyone in the group.

Be supportive and respectful of others as they share their opinions. When conflicts arise, try to respond honestly but also with kindness, patience, and generosity.

Don't force anyone to contribute. People come to faith-sharing groups with different comfort levels. Some are eager to share their most intimate thoughts, while others are reluctant to express their feelings openly. Always make contributing to the discussion voluntary, and never put anyone in a position in which they are forced to respond to a particular question. Chances are that as the sessions progress and the participants get to know one another, shy members will feel more comfortable sharing.

Respect the confidentiality of others. In order to share openly and honestly, participants need to feel confident that what they say won't be repeated outside the group. Make a policy that anything personal shared in the group will stay in the group.

Don't try to "fix" others. This isn't group therapy—it's faith sharing. Your support and compassion can be helpful, but this isn't the appropriate setting to resolve personal problems.

AN INTRODUCTION TO MATTHEW'S GOSPEL

Fr. Joseph A. Mindling, OFM Cap

Fr. Mindling is a Capuchin Franciscan priest and a professor of Sacred Scripture at the Washington Theological Union, a Catholic school of theology and ministry in Washington, DC. He has a doctorate from the Pontifical Biblical Institute. Besides teaching and writing about the Bible, he leads groups of pilgrims to Israel, Greece, and Turkey to deepen their acquaintance with the lands where the Bible was lived and written.

Wouldn't it be exciting if we could interview the writers who first captured the words and deeds of Jesus in the gospels of the New Testament? Perhaps we would come to such an interview with a list of questions that have piqued our curiosity for a long time. Or maybe we would just ask these writers to read the inspired texts out loud to us, adding an explanatory remark here and there. But what would we hope to gain from such an exchange? Some people might desire nothing more than entertainment, like Herod Antipas who tried to impress his courtiers by asking Jesus to perform a miracle. Most of us who love and admire Jesus, however, would simply want to ask what it was like to have known the living Jesus. Not content to just discover new information about the world in which he lived and worked, we would want to ask these writers most of all about Jesus as our friend and savior.

The "Fountain" of Scripture. As far as we know, the four witnesses whose names have become shorthand titles for the gospels have not granted interviews lately. And yet, the dream of learning more from them is more accessible to us than we think. The Vatican II document on divine revelation, *Dei verbum*, tells us that the Scriptures are like a "fountain." This image of a gushing source of clear water reminds us that the inspired word of God in the Bible has something new and refreshing for us, no matter how many times we dip into it.

Jesus promised that the Father would send the Spirit, the Paraclete, to teach us and help us understand more profoundly what he had taught and who he is. "I still have many things to say to you, but you cannot bear them now. When the Spirit of truth comes, he will guide you into all the truth" (John 16:12-13; see also 14:17 and 15:26). When we approach the gospels with an eagerness to receive this truth, we can actually do more than have a dialogue with an evangelist. With the guidance of the Spirit, we can pass from reading about Jesus to a new level of communication with Jesus. Even nonbelievers often find the gospel records of our Lord's life quite interesting, but to those who come with "faith seeking understanding," the reverent reading of the text becomes a place where we find Jesus, and where Jesus finds us.

Unity in Diversity. This introduction aims to help us meet the Messiah in the pages of Matthew's gospel. In modern translations of the Bible, Matthew's gospel holds the honored position as the first book of the New Testament. Its contents include a genealogy of the people and events connected with Jesus' birth, a description of his work and teachings as an adult, and his death and resurrection. Since this sequence sounds similar to the narratives in all the gospels, we might ask the obvious question: Why not dovetail the various stories, fitting together what is unique in each of the four around the "core" that they share? Why not publish devotional meditations based on a hybrid, homogenized "life" of Christ?

This suggestion was addressed in the mid-second century by a text that early church historians call the *Diatessaron*. It states that even though such "gospel harmonies" (as they are called in English) were available, the Christian people opted overwhelmingly for the continued private and liturgical use of the individual gospels. Modern Scripture scholars, still busily discovering fascinating editorial nuances in all four of them, can only applaud the ancient preservation of this wonderful unity in diversity.

No single gospel, nor all the gospels combined, provides us with a detailed account of Jesus' entire earthly life, as would a biography written today. And, unlike contemporary biographers, the evangelists did not focus heavily on a psychological portrait of our Lord. While the church has rightfully and consistently insisted on the historical character of Jesus' words and deeds as reported in the gospels, we know that first-generation Christians knew far more about Jesus than they preserved in writing. The fourth gospel ends with an explicit acknowledgment of this: "But there are also many other things that Jesus did; if every one of them were written down, I suppose that the world itself could not contain the books that would be written" (John 21:25).

On what grounds, then, did the gospel writers decide to include, combine, or omit particular details or episodes? The gospels themselves suggest that the writers worked primarily out of pastoral concerns for their readers. The evangelists wrote, above all, to persuade their readers to accept Jesus in faith, that we might learn more about his earthly mission as it applies to our lives, and that we might continue to deepen in our faith in Jesus through his acts and words. To respond to these texts in the spirit in which they were written, we must approach them today not as biographies but as invitations to deepen our own understanding and personal commitment to our Lord.

Matthew's Gospel. Christian tradition has called the first book in the New Testament the Gospel of Matthew, or simply, Matthew. The official name of this work, the Gospel *According* to Matthew—which we still use in the liturgy today—reminds us that the early church focused much less on the literary task of individual authors than on the authors' connections with the original witnesses of the good news. The oldest testimonies about this gospel identify Matthew with the tax collector whose calling we read about in Matthew 9:9-13 and 10:3. Unfortunately, these precious few verses tell us little that is distinctive about this apostle, and they throw no light on what the words "according to" might have conveyed to ancient readers. On the other hand, what the gospel itself reveals about the community for which it was written can help modern readers enter Matthew's circle of believers and discover what they need to learn about Jesus.

Educated estimates put the composition date around A.D. 80 to 85, a time when relations between church and synagogue were reaching a breaking point. Within this cultural situation, Matthew wrote his gospel for Jewish Christians, who did not view Judaism and Christianity as two contradictory or mutually exclusive religions, as most contemporary Jews and Christians do. On the contrary, Matthew and many of the first converts to Christianity worked zealously to attract other Jewish individuals and families to the way of the Nazarene. At the same time, some of those who rejected Jesus made concerted efforts to denigrate his name, intimidating would-be followers with threats of persecution and expulsion from the religious communities in which many of them had been raised. The Gospel of Matthew was forged in these heated altercations and sometimes even physical violence that accompanied this fierce competition.

Meeting Jesus through Matthew. Although the public polemics have subsided, many of the issues that concerned the early church have never lost their radical religious importance, despite the dramatic differences between first-century Palestine and our world today. Three themes that figure prominently throughout this gospel—and were no doubt important to the people of Matthew's time—can also lead us to a more personal experience of Jesus today.

One of the central themes of the first gospel is the need to understand Jesus as the crowning fulfillment of God's divine initiative begun centuries earlier, starting with the earliest stories found in the Book of Genesis. For Matthew and for us, this salvation history (as we call it today) was not merely a theological theory or a creative interpretation of scriptural history. Jesus was either the Messiah that he claimed to be, or he was a charlatan. Either the God of the covenant had fulfilled his promise to forever maintain a relationship with the descendants of Abraham and Sarah, or God had abandoned his people, which is absurd. Matthew includes more than forty Old Testament quotes in his gospel to continually remind his readers that Jesus was not a last-minute "substitute" for a divine design that had floundered under the weight of human infidelity. Since God had both foreseen and brought about the Christ event, these quotations point to a loving providence that remains constantly faithful throughout the ages to those who accept Jesus as the promised Messiah.

A closely related theme that figures prominently in Matthew's gospel is his vision of individual Christian believers interacting as a community assembled through God's initiative. Many pagans in the first century worked on the premise that religion was essentially a human undertaking, an approach aimed at bribing or placating the forces of nature. Jesus assured us, on the contrary, that "you did not choose me but I chose you" (John 15:16). The special term *ekklesia*, which Matthew uses to express the idea of "church," preserves the emphasis on this divine initiative. In Greek, *ekklesia* means "those called forth." The Old Testament had already adopted this terminology to highlight the status of Israel as God's special people. Its continued use in the New Testament is based on the conviction that Jesus extends membership in the family of faith to all who accept his call. As we pray alongside the Gospel of Matthew, we will learn more and more about God's unflagging interest in how we live, worship, and work together as brothers and sisters. Being "church" means forgiving and being forgiven, seeking the face of Christ among our brothers and sisters, and rediscovering them as members of the family of faith.

A third theme in Matthew's gospel concerns how we grow in our ability to know and praise God through prayer. The earliest converts from Judaism to Christianity faced a serious challenge in discerning how to retain their religious heritage and yet incorporate newness in Christ. The Sermon on the Mount and various other passages throughout this gospel insist on the preservation of the Old Testament and respect for religious leaders—although Jesus does not speak of a blind obedience but of "fulfillment" of the law. As we open ourselves to his teaching, we hope to enter into the spirit of the commandments, moving beyond the "letter" to grasp the way our love for God and for one another shapes all that we do.

These three themes recur throughout the series of short episodes from Jesus' public life that contain important sayings and teachings and seem to provide the structure for Matthew's gospel. But scholars who study Matthew have pointed to a more subtle, underlying rhythm that alternates Jesus' encounters with individuals with his lengthier public discourses, including the Sermon on the Mount (Matthew 5:1–7:29); the Missionary Sermon (10:5-42); the Seven Parables about the Kingdom (13:1-52); the Sermon about Church Life (18:1-35); and the Sermon about the End Times (24:1–25:46). It is through this interplay of public and private glimpses into Jesus' ministry that Jesus' mission and identity unfold.

He Speaks to Our Hearts. There is much opportunity through reading and meditating on the Gospel of Matthew for us to find Jesus and for Jesus to find us. *Dei verbum*, the Vatican II document on divine revelation, closes with an exhortation to accompany all of our Scripture reading with prayer. This is welcome advice, but we must remember that prayer is a two-way communication.

An interesting illustration of this fact took place several years ago when a representative from the International Bible Society went to interview the leader of a tribal group in the mountains of Central America. After years of listening to Spanish translations of the New Testament, the people in this area had finally been able to hear the words of the gospels in their own language, a Mayan dialect used by relatively few people. When the visiting scholar questioned the chief about the experience of hearing Jesus' words in his own tongue, the question prompted a thought-provoking reply. "It is wonderful," the man said, "but now Jesus is always telling me what to do." Something like this will happen to all of us when we open the Scriptures and speak to the Jesus we find there. He does more than listen. He speaks to our hearts.

WALKING WITH JESUS IN THE HOLY LAND

Fr. Joseph A. Mindling, OFM Cap

Among the greatest treasures bequeathed to us by the authors of the New Testament are their descriptions of the last days of Jesus' public ministry, climaxing in his brutal execution and his triumphant victory over death. Although Jesus' death and resurrection are the very center of our faith, most of us tend to think of them as abstract realities, giving little thought to the actual places where those events occurred. Yet for Jesus' companions, the locations where each event took place at the end of their Master's life added significance to what he did—the colonnaded outer porches of the temple, the barracks where Roman soldiers tortured prisoners, the dusty narrow streets of Jerusalem, the City of David (see John 10:22-39; Mark 15:1-20).

Jesus invited us to take up our cross and follow him (see Mark 8:34). One approach that can help us follow in our Redeemer's footsteps focuses on revisiting the actual sites where he most tangibly demonstrated his love for us. This centuries-old practice of pilgrimage has inspired many generations of believers to undertake a journey to the Holy Land. From this practice came the tradition of praying the Stations of the Cross. For a few minutes, let us reappropriate this tradition as well, pondering some of what we know about those places that Jesus sanctified by making them part of our salvation history.

The Temple. All four gospels describe our Lord's preaching, debating, and performing healings in the temple in Jerusalem in the days leading up to his arrest. This grand edifice, still being embellished by artisans as part of Herod's remodeling project, was the most impressive Jewish place of worship in the world. Comparable in size and beauty to the marble monuments of the Greeks and the Romans, it was also considered the holiest spot on earth. Its glistening facade of white marble and gold represented the presence of divine glory among the people. Its clouds of sacrificial smoke and rising choruses of praise symbolized the reverence that Israel owed to the God of the covenant. Yet Jesus spoke of his own body as the prototypical temple that would rise up, even as the walls of the old sanctuary would fall. Through the paschal mystery, Jesus transforms us into temples of the new covenant (see John 2:13-25; 1 Corinthians 6:19).

The Cenacle. Christian tradition places the site of the Last Supper in a section of Jerusalem—on the southwestern ridge of the city—where well-to-do priestly families resided, well cared for by their domestics. Jesus obviously picked an upper room "in the right neighborhood" to officiate as high priest of the new covenant and to wash his friends' feet as servant of the servants of God. Ironically, this same "respectable" quarter of the city, the area medieval pilgrims called Mount Zion, was where many believe the priest Annas lived and where Jesus was brought back for secret, illegal interrogations (see Luke 22:7-13; Matthew 26:57-68).

The Mount of Olives. The agony Jesus suffered in the garden prior to his arrest is remembered today on the eastern side of Jerusalem in a shrine church near the bottom of a slope, much of which is covered by Jewish cemeteries and olive trees, some of them ancient. This area has maintained its popularity as a burial place in part because it is identified with the Valley of Jehoshaphat, which the Book of Joel associates with an apocalyptic conclusion to history as we know it (see Joel 3:2, 12, 14). The name Gethsemane, meaning "oil press," has suggested to Christian artists the presence of a gnarled and leafy orchard, lending seclusion and greater darkness to the hillside in the late evening. Imagine Jesus slipping away from the hustle and heat of the city to find time here to collect his thoughts and pray. How appropriate that the conqueror of death should engage the enemy in a place dotted with so many monuments to seemingly invincible mortality (see Mark 14:32-52; Luke 22:39-53).

The Courtrooms. The evangelists described Jesus' arraignment before the high priests Annas and Caiaphas, the Sanhedrin, King Herod, and Pontius Pilate. Archeological remains and ancient written descriptions suggest that the atmosphere in Palestinian courtrooms would have had much in common with judicial proceedings under any dictatorship. The gospel accounts reflect the trappings of bureaucracy and politically determined outcomes carried out in solemn, official surroundings, with officious personnel, posturing judges, and an innocent defendant accepting the inevitability of a guilty verdict. Bystanders howl out their hostility or, worse, look on in silence (see Mark 14:53–15:15; John 18:12–19:16).

Golgotha. After receiving his unjust sentence of public execution, Jesus was humiliated by being paraded through the narrow, crowded streets of a city busy preparing for the most important feast of the year. Many of the foreign visitors would have considered the whole business of the Nazarene's crucifixion an unwelcome intrusion into their high holy day festivities. Jesus' cross and those of the criminals executed with him were raised on a mound in a basin-like depression, the site of a long-abandoned stone quarry. Jesus, marginalized by the religious establishment, was raised up on a natural pedestal, a stone, which the construction workers had rejected and which reminded the popular imagination of a skull (see Matthew 21:42; Psalm 118:22).

Not far from this outcropping, certain individuals had paid dearly to have burial chambers carved into the sloping walls of the quarry. Minor landscaping changes had lent an air of respectability to a resting place for the wealthy, conveniently (and legally) located just outside the city walls. How tempting it must have been for the Roman occupation authorities to insult the Jewish populace by using this hallowed spot for the execution of controversial criminals! It is no wonder, too, that Mary Magdalene presumed that anyone out early on the first working day of the week would be part of the gardening cleanup staff (see Luke 23:26-56; John 19:17-42).

Because of the natural human aversion to psychological and physical pain, successive retelling of what happened during Jesus' final days might well have tended to abbreviate the accounts of our Lord's suffering and to expand the reports of his successes and later vindication. However, the Christian community obviously recognized from the beginning the great spiritual value of revisiting the saving events of the first Christian Passover. Instead of letting this sacred memory fade, the Spirit moved the writers and readers of the New Testament to preserve these sacred moments. The same Holy Spirit has enabled Christian people in every age and place to understand the narratives of Jesus' pain and victory as living springs of spiritual strength and inspiration. Western painters and Eastern iconographers, liturgists and hymn writers, mystics and penitents—we all draw on these chapters to experience what Jesus meant when he prophesied, "And I, when I am lifted up from the earth, will draw all people to myself" (John 12:32).

Matthew 1:1-17: God's Extraordinary Plan

While the inclusion of Jesus' genealogy may seem tedious to us today, it establishes Jesus' place within the Jewish tradition and his continuity with great Old Testament figures. It also highlights the Father's deliberate preparation for the sending of the Son. God carefully unfolded his plan by using his people across the generations—some admirable and some not.

Bible scholars have long commented on the "irregularities" found in Matthew's genealogy, especially its inclusion of women, an unusual occurrence in Jewish genealogies of that time. St. Jerome said that Matthew chose sinful women for his list, such as Rahab, but this doesn't accurately explain Ruth's inclusion. Others have said that Matthew chose foreign women, which is true of Tamar, Rahab, and Ruth. Still others have commented that their "irregularity" is the very thing the women in Matthew have in common. Yet each also played an extraordinary part in the history of Israel. They thus prepared the way for the unique and extraordinary role of Mary, the virgin mother of Jesus.

God worked in all of these unique individuals to prepare for the coming of his Son. We can find encouragement in this fact. Whether we are high and mighty or lowly and limited, God invites us and uses us to bring Jesus to others, just as Mary brought him to us. However "irregular" we may consider ourselves, the Father lets nothing stand in the way of his love, not even ourselves. What joyful hope this instills in us, that God uses us in an extraordinary way to bring his Son to others! In this sense, we participate in the ongoing genealogy of Christ.

1. Which names do you recognize from Matthew's list? Whose story are you most familiar with, and how does that story add to your understanding of Jesus?

_____

_____

_____

2. If you could create your own Christian genealogy, who would you include in your list? What individuals or groups have most significantly influenced your own walk with Christ?

_____

_____

_____

3. Do you know anyone who feels alienated from the church because of events in his or her past? What could you do to show them that God loves them and welcomes them back?

_____

_____

_____

Matthew 1:18-25: Obedient and Dedicated Faith

Joseph demonstrated what can happen when we cooperate with God. Even before an angel had spoken to him, he had determined to protect Mary at great risk to his own standing in the community. Based on her testimony that she was "with child from the Holy Spirit" (Matthew 1:18), he trusted God and chose what he considered to be the safest course of action for her. An angel then further enlightened him by confirming Mary's words and rewarding Joseph's trust, saying, "[Jesus] will save his people from their sins" (1:21).

Joseph believed in God's plan and worked to see it fulfilled; thus, the Messiah was born. The wonder and glory of all God's promises came to fruition in part through the cooperation of this humble and upright man. In a unique way, he anticipated St. Paul's words that through Christ "we have received grace and apostleship to bring about the obedience of faith" (Romans 1:5). Joseph clearly demonstrated that "obedience of faith"; he simply trusted in God and opened himself to the grace that God gave him.

Through baptism, we have received grace and apostleship. We have been called to the obedience of faith—not to a slavish obedience based on fear and anxiety, but to a joyful obedience based on simple trust and love. Through joyful obedience, we cooperate with God in his desire to bring all people into his kingdom. He teaches us to dedicate our whole being—body, mind, and soul—to an active Christian faith. As we respond to that call, we will see marvelous things take place—as did Joseph.

1. What thoughts might have gone through Joseph's mind when Mary told him about her condition? What demands were placed on Joseph by his trusting and cooperating with God's plan for him? What graces do you think he received by trusting in God?

_____

_____

_____

2. Recall a time when you were confused or anxious about an issue. How did you resolve it? Were you quick to ask for God's guidance, or did you hesitate, or did you not ask at all?

_____

_____

_____

3. What habits and attitudes can you develop in your day-to-day life that will help make you more able to cooperate with God in the future? How might trusting God without reservation open you to receive more of his grace?

_____

_____

_____

Matthew 2:1-12: Gifts for the King

After humanity's devastating fall from grace into sin, after centuries of preparation, war, exile, prophecy, and longing, the eternal Son of God manifested himself to the nations through a lowly birth to a humble Jewish couple. As the light of salvation dawned on the earth, wise men from other nations came to pay homage to the one in whom all wisdom and dominion and power is found.

This revelation of Christ in the world must have been powerful indeed. Sages from the East, men of learning, were drawn to him! What could have induced them to leave their homes and positions of prominence to go on such a long journey? Only a work of God in their hearts could have moved them to recognize the one they came to worship.

The Fathers of the church held that the sages' gifts revealed their full recognition of Jesus. They brought gold as tribute for a king, incense to burn in praise of God, and myrrh to soothe the sufferings of humanity. These three gifts signal Jesus' authority, deity, and future suffering and death, which would bring about the salvation of all God's people.

What fruit was borne from the journey of these wise men! In their wake, generations of wise people continue to bow down before the humble child of Nazareth. Like the wealth of the nations in the prophet's words (see Isaiah 60:5), men and women from every age have laid their treasures before Christ, renouncing the apparent wealth of this world to embrace the real wealth that is found in repentance, humility, and faith.

1. How did the various groups of people in this passage react to the news of the newborn king of the Jews? Which group or groups do you most closely identify with? Why?

_____

_____

_____

2. What worldly treasure do you feel compelled to give away to Christ? What spiritual treasure do you wish to offer Christ?

_____

_____

_____

3. Why do you think Jesus came to earth in such humble circumstances? How can his birth influence your perception of circumstances in your own life?

_____

_____

_____

Matthew 2:13-23: Joseph, the Father Figure

The fact that an angel spoke to Joseph (see Matthew 1:20; 2:13) and warned him of impending danger emphasized the importance of the message and the need for it to be heeded. Joseph heard God's word because he was not only a "righteous man" (1:19) but also a loving, faithful man of God. His heart was open to hearing God's message!

As foster father and protector of the long-awaited Messiah, Joseph can be viewed as a model parent and as one who can teach us much about faith-filled family life. Today, no less than in biblical times, parents and those in parental roles need to hear from God. This involves a special commitment to prayer and Scripture reading. God wants us to know that the Holy Spirit, who dwells in each of us, can teach us how to nurture our families and loved ones. The gifts of the Spirit, including wisdom, understanding, counsel, and knowledge (see Isaiah 11:2; 1 Corinthians 12:7-11), can help us shepherd our families along the way of the Lord.

Empowered by the wisdom of God, Joseph could see the forces of evil in the world (personified by Herod) and took steps to protect his son from them. We, too, need to protect our children from the real threats of the world. We know that protecting our children doesn't mean hiding them from reality; it means teaching and training them in the ways of God. If we protect and teach our children—especially in the formative years—they will gain the ability to make decisions based on gospel truths.

1. In what ways did Joseph secure his wife's and son's safety? How might those actions have been difficult for him?

_____

_____

_____

2. Have you ever felt called by God to do things for your family that you considered difficult? How did you respond?

_____

_____

_____

3. What parenting or caregiving lessons does Joseph teach you? What can you do to help create environments and opportunities for teaching gospel truths to children?

_____

_____

_____

Matthew 3:1-12: Repentance and the Spirit's Guidance

Preaching in the desert of Judea, John the Baptist spoke a simple but difficult message to all who came to be baptized: "Repent, for the kingdom of heaven has come near. . . . 'Prepare the way of the Lord, make his paths straight'" (Matthew 3:2, 3). John understood that repentance and spiritual conversion would be essential for receiving salvation through the coming Messiah.

Today we still hear John's message calling us to change our behavior and set our hearts on God. How willing are we to let God change not only aspects of our behavior but also our whole lives? Will we allow the Holy Spirit to reveal to us the sinful habits and thought patterns that act as barriers to God's work in our lives?

John's message calls us to examine the root causes of our pride and selfishness. He calls us to strike at the root of our resentments and grudges that cause division in our families, communities, and parish relationships. Most of us know that this task is too difficult to handle on our own.

Through baptism we receive help from the Holy Spirit, the Spirit of power and new life. The Spirit actively helps us draw closer to God and share more fully in his divine life. Therefore, the Spirit does not only reveal our sins but also guides us into the life God intended for us as his sole creation made in his own image and likeness. God wants us to lead our lives as privileged sharers in his divine life.

1. What does John's lifestyle say about his understanding of God? Why do you think so many people responded to his message?

   _____

   _____

   _____

2. When you read John's words, "Repent, for the kingdom of heaven has come near" (Matthew 3:2), what attitudes and actions of yours come most quickly to mind? Do you feel a sense of urgency in repenting? Why or why not?

   _____

   _____

   _____

3. What one or more things can you request from the Holy Spirit to help you prepare for Christ to come more fully into your life?

   _____

   _____

   _____

Matthew 3:13-17: The Servant's Baptism

After years of waiting and preparing, Jesus recognized that the time had come for him to begin his mission. No longer would he remain hidden away in Nazareth, quietly plying his trade as a carpenter. The day had arrived for him to play his part in the Father's plan.

Jesus began his public ministry not in glory but in humility, as he submitted himself to a baptism of repentance. He, the sinless one, heeded the Baptizer's call to sinners; this was in order to "fulfill all righteousness" (Matthew 3:15). And when Jesus came up out of the water, the Spirit descended on him and the Father testified to him, declaring him to be "my Son, the Beloved" and that he was "well pleased" with him (3:17).

By recounting Jesus' baptism in this way, Matthew emphasized Jesus' role as the servant of the Lord. Yes, Jesus had come to bring justice, to open blind eyes, and to release prisoners (see Isaiah 42:3, 7), but even more important, Jesus had come to give himself as a sin offering, to bear others' sins and intercede for their forgiveness (see 53:10, 12).

St. Paul said that through baptism we are baptized into Christ (see Romans 6:3; Galatians 3:27). We, therefore, affirm that as the Spirit descended upon Jesus at his baptism, the Spirit also descended upon us at our baptisms. As the Father declared Jesus to be his beloved Son, God also declares us to be his beloved sons and daughters in Christ. And like Jesus, we, too, are called to give our lives as servants of the kingdom.

1. How would you rephrase, in your own words, Jesus' understanding of his need for baptism (see Matthew 3:15)?

_____

_____

_____

2. Do you have any fears or reservations about sharing in the baptism of Christ? If so, consider listing them and asking God to remove these barriers from your life.

_____

_____

_____

3. In baptism we were made sons and daughters of our heavenly Father. How can an awareness of this reality make a difference in your day-to-day life?

_____

_____

_____

Matthew 4:1-11: Deliverance from Temptation

Satan's temptations of Jesus reveal the three key ways in which Satan works. First, he attempts to persuade us to use spiritual power and authority to benefit ourselves. For example, Satan tempts people serving in the church to use their positions of authority for self-aggrandizement. Second, he attempts to persuade us to bargain with God, perhaps enticing us to convince God to give us favors in exchange for our prayers or services. Third, Satan attempts to deceive us into worshipping idols, such as money, fame, possessions, or status, instead of God.

The Prince of Darkness wants us to act on his temptations, to turn away from God. Will we succumb to Satan and his seemingly logical arguments, or will we renounce him and choose obedience to the Father? Yielding to Satan, even in small matters, invites great danger. Satan completely opposes God; Satan wants nothing more than the destruction of all who follow Christ.

We are not alone in our efforts to resist Satan. Paul said, "The free gift in the grace of the one man, Jesus Christ, abounded for the many" (Romans 5:15). The Letter to the Hebrews says, "Because he himself was tested by what he suffered, [Jesus] is able to help those who are being tested" (2:18). Because Jesus was tested as we are and triumphed, we, too, can share in his victory. Because he destroyed the work of the devil (1 John 3:8) by his death to sin and resurrection to new life, he has won protection and deliverance for all of us who die to sin and rise with him in faith.

1. What do you think was Satan's goal in tempting Jesus? What impresses you most about Jesus' refusal to succumb to these temptations?

_____

_____

_____

2. Of the three key ways in which Satan most often works, which do you personally find most difficult to resist? How would knowledge of Satan's tactics help you battle such temptations in the future?

_____

_____

_____

3. How does Jesus' free gift of grace—that is, forgiveness of your sins and your justification before God—affect your faith in him to help you overcome future temptations?

_____

_____

_____

Matthew 4:12-25: The Christian Mission

Following the arrest of John the Baptist, Jesus returned to Galilee and began his public ministry. He called the apostles to share in his ministry by sending them out to "fish for people" (Matthew 4:19). As Jesus had done, they began "teaching in their synagogues and proclaiming the good news of the kingdom and curing every disease and every sickness among the people" (4:23).

The mission begun by Jesus in Galilee had become his followers' responsibility. "From that time Jesus began to proclaim, 'Repent, for the kingdom of heaven has come near'" (Matthew 4:17). This kingdom shone out before men "in the word, in the works, and in the presence of Christ" (Vatican II, *Dogmatic Constitution on the Church*, 5).

As members of the body of Christ, we have all been called to participate in the mission that Jesus entrusted to the church. Throughout our lives, we will have many opportunities to proclaim the gospel, teach others about our faith, and pray expectantly for physical, emotional, or spiritual healing. As we do so, we reveal Jesus, the Son of God, and extend his kingdom on earth. Let us not allow fear, complacency, or doubts about God's power to block us from becoming vessels of the grace of Christ.

1. What does the readiness of the apostles to leave behind their livelihoods and families say about Jesus? What does it say about their faith in Jesus?

_____

_____

_____

2. How can we best overcome the fears and doubts that hold us back and prevent us from revealing Christ to the world?

_____

_____

_____

3. In what ways might God be calling you to participate in his mission in the world? What areas of your life might you be willing to abandon in order to more fully respond to that call?

_____

_____

_____

Matthew 5:1-12: Abundant Blessings

How jarring the beatitudes must have sounded to the people who first heard Jesus speak them! How can the poor and meek, the merciful and pure in heart, even the persecuted, consider themselves happy? Many of us naturally recoil from such ideas, as Jesus' audience surely did.

The Greek word for "blessed"—*makarios*—has two meanings in Scripture. First, the "blessed" one receives divine favor, and, second, this person is "happy" or "fortunate." In the beatitudes, Jesus combined these meanings, giving us a road map to help us find not only happiness, but also the blessings and grace of God in our lives.

Jesus was often misunderstood, and many people treated him with suspicion or, worse, with violence. Yet Jesus was filled with overflowing peace and joy. Why? Jesus teaches us to entrust ourselves to God, and he invites us to experience the blessings that flow from such trust. We entrust ourselves to God by becoming like Jesus: poor in spirit, meek, merciful, hungry for righteousness, and pure in heart. Furthermore, he gives us his Holy Spirit to guide and empower us to follow this path. His life within us will always bring us overflowing peace and joy.

When Jesus described the rewards of such a life, he used the future tense, because he wanted to extend our vision beyond our earthly life to the kingdom he had come to inaugurate. In the kingdom, we *will* find comfort, we *will* be filled, we *will* receive mercy, and we *will* see God (see Matthew 5:4-8).

1. How do the beatitudes compare and contrast with the attitudes you find in contemporary culture?

   _____

   _____

   _____

2. Which beatitude do you identify with the most? Which the least? Why?

   _____

   _____

   _____

3. What would true happiness look like in your life? How would taking on the characteristics in the beatitudes bring you closer to this vision?

   _____

   _____

   _____

Matthew 5:13-16: Salt of the Earth, Light of the World

Jesus said, "You are the salt of the earth .... You are the light of the world" (Matthew 5:13, 14). Considering the condition and status of his followers, Jesus' pronouncement must have surely startled them. While a few notables or scholars may have been in attendance, most of the people who had gathered on the mountainside to listen to Jesus were society's poor, sick, uneducated, and relatively unimportant.

Standing before all of these people, Jesus defined the role of discipleship. Just as salt makes food taste better, it also preserves it. In a similar way, Jesus called his followers to witness to the truth and to sustain it. And in the same way that a small oil lamp in those days provided a home with its sole source of evening light, Jesus told the disciples to be the sole source of light in a darkened world. They were to accomplish this by being reflections of the one who said, "I am the light of the world" (John 8:12).

Jesus did not tell his disciples that doing good works would earn them salvation. Rather, he said that the works they did would be proclamations of the faith in their hearts. Just as it is the very nature of salt to flavor and preserve, so it is the very nature of light to shine and illuminate what is around it. Similarly, it is the nature of Jesus' disciples to reflect his light to a darkened world in order for all to see, know, and glorify the Father in heaven.

1. How does salt lose its taste? What does it mean for a person to lose the "saltiness" in his or her spiritual life? How can we preserve our "flavor"?

_____

_____

_____

2. Are there any darkened corners in your personal life in which you haven't allowed the light of Christ to shine through? If so, how could you open those corners to Christ?

_____

_____

_____

3. In what ways do you shine the light of Christ out to the world? Can you think of any ways that your light could shine more brightly?

_____

_____

_____

Matthew 5:17-19: Fulfilling the Law and the Prophets

In the Old Testament, God revealed himself and gave direction through the law and the prophets. In the Ten Commandments, given to Moses on Mount Sinai (see Exodus 20), and through all the major and minor prophets that we find in Scripture, God spoke his word to his chosen people.

Then, as the Word of God became flesh, Jesus *fulfilled* all that God had spoken through the law and prophets. To be clear, Jesus came "not to abolish [the law] but to fulfill [it]" and said that anyone who relaxed even "the least of these commandments . . . will be called least in the kingdom of heaven" (Matthew 5:17, 19). He came to "fulfill," that is, to perfect the unperfected. Matthew's gospel identifies six major categories in which Jesus perfected the law: murder, adultery, divorce, oaths, revenge, and love of enemies (see 5:21-48).

Through his death and resurrection, Jesus opened up to us the possibility of authentically living the fullness of the law and the prophets. He stressed the supreme good of the way of life set forth by the original law and the prophets, but he further taught that only through a living faith in him by the power of the Holy Spirit can we live it out. We must humbly acknowledge that on our own merits we are unable to keep the law. Only by faith and baptism into Jesus' death and resurrection do we receive the power to live new life in obedience to the Father.

1. When Jesus referred to "the law," what law and which aspects of that law did he mean to fulfill? And why did he bring it up in this context (see Matthew 5)?

   _____

   _____

   _____

2. How can we best avoid the trap of legalism—of focusing on obeying every rule but failing to carry out its spirit? Why is Jesus calling his people to go beyond a legalistic view of the law and the prophets?

   _____

   _____

   _____

3. Think of an area in your life where you struggle to be obedient to God's will. How can the Holy Spirit empower you this week to become obedient in this area?

   _____

   _____

   _____

Matthew 5:20-26: Reconciling with One Another

Hardly a day goes by that we don't hear in the news of another robbery. These crimes appall us, and with self-righteous attitudes, we condemn the thief before God. This self-righteousness is not too unlike that of the Pharisees and the scribes. Jesus said that unless our righteousness exceeded that of the scribes and Pharisees, we would never enter the kingdom of heaven (Matthew 5:20). He meant that being right with God depends not only on refraining from acts prohibited by the law but also on directing our hearts in loving relationships with God and neighbor.

Instead of feeling self-satisfied for not being thieves, let us examine our hearts for anger and resentment toward others. These attitudes violate the greatest commandments that Jesus taught us: love of God and love of neighbor (see Matthew 22:37-39). Instead, Jesus taught us the proper response to our brothers and sisters: repent and be reconciled (see 5:24). It is not enough to say, "I should not be angry with my spouse or child or teacher. I should not be jealous of my co-worker. I should not resent my boss for correcting me or not appreciating me enough." The kingdom of heaven calls for reconciliation, not just an acknowledgment of wrongful thoughts or acts.

In a talk given in the Netherlands in 1985, Pope John Paul II put it this way: "External observance of the law has no great value if the heart is blind or wicked. . . . The heart, in other words the conscience, must be purified and informed. . . . Christ reveals to his disciples that here is a value that surpasses all others and binds them together: Love. This law of love, which contains the Law and the Prophets, must become the law of their conscience."

1. Jesus taught us to seek reconciliation with loved ones prior to offering gifts to God (see Matthew 5:23-24). What does this suggest to you about God's priorities?

_____

_____

_____

2. In what ways do you think Jesus is calling you to exceed the righteousness of the scribes and Pharisees? How can you best inform and purify your heart as Pope John Paul II said?

_____

_____

_____

3. What conflicts can you end today or in the near future simply by seeking reconciliation rather than making "federal cases" out of them?

_____

_____

_____

Matthew 5:27-32: Grace-Filled Marriage

Matthew carefully arranged his gospel to portray Jesus as the Messiah who inaugurates the long-awaited kingdom of God. In the Sermon on the Mount, Matthew presented Jesus inviting his listeners to enter this kingdom. Jesus first described the kingdom's unique blessings—the beatitudes. Then, like a new Moses, he introduced a series of intrinsic principles characterizing the messianic reign.

Ultimately, Jesus shifted the focus of our religious commitments from the legalities of the law to the innermost drives of the heart. He did this by using the challenges we face in our daily lives and employing a rabbinical style of discourse: "You have heard that it was said . . . but I say to you . . ." (Matthew 5:21-48). Additionally, Jesus' vision transcended the letter of the law. The Old Testament command, "You shall not commit adultery," becomes, "Everyone who looks at a woman with lust has already committed adultery with her in his heart" (5:28). Jesus even suggested that believers might even be better off sacrificing eyes or limbs—meaning that we should be ready to let go of anything that could put us in the way of offending God—to gain the kingdom (see 5:29-30).

Jesus' teaching on divorce, for example, shattered the natural preconceptions held by those who heard him (witness the disciples' protests in Matthew 19:10). Jesus did not intend to condemn husbands and wives to loveless and possibly destructive marriages; on the contrary, he revealed the grace God gives married couples to live in a way that advances the kingdom of God. Like the beatitudes and the call to love our enemies, all these teachings revealed a radically different way of life inaugurated by Jesus.

1. Why do you think Jesus extended these laws beyond their original legal definitions? What point was he trying to make?

_____

_____

_____

2. What habits and preoccupations in your own life could use an infusion of divine grace to help you behave and think differently?

_____

_____

_____

3. What attitudes and behaviors can husbands and wives adopt to help them avoid the pitfalls of adultery and divorce? What attitudes and behaviors can help single men and women live chastely?

_____

_____

_____

Matthew 5:33-37: Practicing Personal Integrity

The Old Testament clearly allowed oath taking: "And you shall not swear falsely by my name, profaning the name of your God" (Leviticus 19:12). How startling, then, must Jesus' words have sounded to his listeners! He taught them to not make oaths at all, especially those that invoke God's name and all that he rules—heaven and earth, Jerusalem, even one's own "head" (Matthew 5:34-37).

Instead, Jesus calls us to a higher standard of trustworthiness, one in which our word can be depended on without the necessity of an oath. Good relationships rest on the foundation stones of trust and integrity. Where mutual trust and personal integrity exist, relationships grow strong and deep. On the other hand, when we prove ourselves untrustworthy by not doing what we say we will do, we stifle opportunities to love our spouses, family members, friends, neighbors, and even the strangers in our midst.

Our trustworthiness and integrity regarding gospel standards act together as a powerful witness to a skeptical world. When we call ourselves followers of Christ, we say, in effect, that we follow the standards Christ established. We bear witness to these standards with faith-filled words and actions. We must honestly recognize, therefore, that we need Christ's life within us to sustain our trustworthiness and spiritual integrity. In Christ, by the power of the Holy Spirit, we come to know our shortcomings and the way that leads us into all truth (see John 16:7-13).

1. If Jesus didn't want us to swear oaths at all, what does this suggest to you about his opinion of our ability to keep our word? What is the essence of his teaching?

_____

_____

_____

2. What happens in a relationship when a person is not honest about how he or she really feels? If you have ever experienced such a relationship, what did you do about it?

_____

_____

_____

3. How can you get into the habit of simply answering yes or no when asked to make a commitment or perform a task? How best can you ensure that you will follow through on your commitment?

_____

_____

_____

Matthew 5:38-42: Forgiveness Rather Than Retaliation

At first glance, the Old Testament teaching about revenge (an eye for an eye and a tooth for a tooth—see Exodus 21:24) seems vindictive. In fact, however, God gave this law to prevent people from inflicting punishment or retribution greater than the offense that evoked it. This teaching on revenge is the fifth example Matthew used to illustrate Jesus' statement that he came to fulfill the law and the prophets, not abolish them (see Matthew 5:17).

This new teaching of forgiveness rather than revenge was—and still is—difficult to accept. It runs counter to all that we, as fallen men and women, have in our hearts concerning how to relate to others. When we are wronged, we want to retaliate. We want revenge. We want justice. Our focus on *revenge* and *justice* causes separation between ourselves and our brothers and sisters.

Jesus died on the cross so that all people could be united in one body—his body. He wants his people to live in unity. In order for this to occur, however, we need to obey God's command to love him and to love one another. This command, most perfectly lived out by Jesus, is our first obligation as sons and daughters of God (see Matthew 22:37-39).

When someone wrongs us, we must learn to respond from the heart—in a way that shows we believe that Jesus died on the cross for everyone and that his victory is stronger than our hunger for revenge. We can then ask God for the grace to forgive, to return evil with good. The more we live this teaching, the more God's love will grow within us.

1. Do you think Jesus literally wants you to turn the other cheek if someone were to strike you? In all situations? Does this teaching challenge you? Why or why not?

_____

_____

_____

2. What is your initial reaction when an injustice is done to you? Do you retaliate or offer peace and love? What would help you to respond in a more Christlike way?

_____

_____

_____

3. What dispositions and attitudes could you develop in advance that would help you to respond lovingly the next time you suffer an injustice? How would faith in the awesome power of Christ's love for all his people help?

_____

_____

_____

Matthew 5:43-48: Love for Enemies

The eternal Father looked down from heaven, and compassion filled his heart. He saw the misery of sin that had overtaken the people he had created. Out of love for his creation, God sent his Son, Jesus, to live and die for us that we might be restored to him. How it must bring joy to the Father and the risen Son to send the Holy Spirit, the love of God poured out, to those who are joined to Jesus through faith and baptism!

God's love pours out to those who believe—love that is divine, infinite, eternal, deep. This love, through faith in Christ, allows us to love beyond our human limitations. By the power of the Holy Spirit, we can love not only those who love us but also our enemies—even those who persecute us.

Jesus taught, "Be perfect . . . as your heavenly Father is perfect" (Matthew 5:48). This perfection has to do with our ability to be like Jesus and to love as he loved. This unselfish love of God always desires the best for our brothers and sisters. This love transforms us from within.

How do we recognize this love in our lives? In an effort to assess our love, we can ask the following questions: Have we hurt our spouse, our children, or our parents through our unloving ways? Have we loved those in authority over us? Have we loved our neighbors—in our churches, communities, and around the world? Have we loved those who are poor or defenseless? Remember, the degree to which we are open to God's love is the degree to which we love others.

1. Do you believe that you can be perfect as God is perfect? Is simple love for an enemy a perfection? Explain.

_____

_____

_____

2. Write down your list of "enemies." How might you love each person on your list?

_____

_____

_____

3. How might a regular time of prayer each day make you more loving? What about more frequent reception of the sacraments, especially reconciliation and the Eucharist?

_____

_____

_____

Matthew 6:1-6, 16-18: The Motives of Charity

Jesus admonished his followers not to perform charitable deeds, such as prayer, fasting, and almsgiving, in the way the hypocrites did (see Matthew 6:16). The word "hypocrite" in Greek means "actor," one who performs in front of others, pretending to be something he or she is not. A spiritual hypocrite is one whose motivation for pious conduct is self-glorification.

Prayer, fasting, and almsgiving—if humanly motivated—tend to draw attention to ourselves. If we seek recognition for these practices or do them to show our holiness, they are good ways to inflate the ego. Performing charitable deeds out of love for God, however, brings great joy and healing to our lives. The fruitfulness of our works of charity depends on our ability to put aside preoccupations with self.

The *Catechism of the Catholic Church* says,

"The New Law is called a *law of love* because it makes us act out of the love infused by the Holy Spirit, . . . a *law of grace*, because it confers the strength of grace to act, by means of faith and the sacraments; a *law of freedom*, because it sets us free from the ritual and juridical observances of the Old Law" (1972).

Jesus was always one with the Father and acted for the Father's honor, not seeking attention or public glory for himself. Through a living, personal relationship with Jesus and his divine grace, we, too, can practice true charity. Mother Teresa said, "We must be aware of oneness with Christ, as he was aware of oneness with his Father. Our activity is truly apostolic only insofar as we permit him to work in us and through us with his power, with his desire, and with his love" (*Gift from God*).

1. Prayer, fasting, and almsgiving are time-honored religious practices. Why do you think that they can be so helpful to our growth in holiness? How can we avoid the trap of hypocrisy?

_____

_____

_____

2. In what ways can you give alms, pray, and fast without drawing attention to yourself? Try to name at least one way for each of these three activities.

_____

_____

_____

3. Who will you give alms to next? Who will you pray for? What will you pray for? When is your next fast? Will anyone know you're doing these things?

_____

_____

_____

Matthew 6:7-15: Prayer of the Heart

Consider the prevailing attitudes of Jesus' contemporaries toward God: they knew him as all-powerful, all-knowing, and all-caring. They believed that he created the world and all that lived, delivered them from slavery, gave them a homeland, and provided for their needs. They revered his name, YHWH—or Yahweh in English—and held it to be so sacred that they dared not even pronounce it.

Then along came Jesus. When his disciples asked him to teach them how to pray, he began by addressing God as "Abba," the rough equivalent of "Dad." Jesus had not only given his disciples a new title for Yahweh, but he had also revealed that, as a result of his incarnation and his forthcoming death and resurrection, all of God's people would henceforth relate to God in a totally new way—as their beloved Father.

We call God our "Father" because he has adopted us as his children in Christ, the Son. Because the Holy Spirit dwells in us (the very same Spirit who dwells in Jesus), we are brought to true spiritual life in God. We share in the very holiness of Jesus, and thus we say with him, "Abba."

Prayer consists of words and dispositions of our heart. The whole of the Lord's Prayer springs from a loving relationship with God. When our hearts know God in this intimate way, we bless his name and long for the coming of his kingdom. We ask that God's will be done on earth. We ask God to provide for our daily needs. And as trusting children, we beg our loving Father to ward off temptation and to protect us from the evil one. In doing so, we come to know Almighty God as Abba.

1. What did Jesus mean by "empty phrases" (Matthew 6:7)? How are empty phrases unlike the Lord's Prayer?

_____

_____

_____

2. Why do you think the Lord's Prayer is the perfect model for our whole prayer life? How can it become the foundation of our daily peace and joy?

_____

_____

_____

3. What do you take away from this passage and meditation regarding how or how not to pray?

_____

_____

_____

Matthew 6:19-23: Treasures in Heaven

Jesus knew that material possessions lose their luster; they never fulfill the deepest longings of our hearts. Yet we cling desperately to the thought that if only we satisfy our desires, the longings will go away. While God has created us with these desires, he has also created us with hearts to love and to be loved. Only when we fill our hearts with the treasure of God's love will our ultimate longings be satisfied.

St. Athanasius (c. 296–373) wrote in his account of the life of St. Antony of Egypt (c. 251–356) that Antony was challenged by Jesus' words on wealth: he felt that "the words of the Gospel had been directed to him. He hurried out and made a gift of his inheritance . . . to the villagers for he did not want himself and his sister to be held back by property. He sold the rest of his goods and gave the money to the poor, except for a small sum which he reserved for his sister" (*Life of St. Antony*).

Antony took the words of the gospel literally. He realized that material possessions had obstructed his walk with the Lord, obscuring his spiritual vision of God. While most of us have responsibilities that prevent us from giving away everything as Antony did, we can still become "poor in spirit" (Matthew 5:3). By dedicating our lives to the Lord and his call for us, rather than focusing on earthly treasures, we become more generous with our time and money. With spiritual eyes, we see the uselessness of acquiring "things," and we instead seek the enduring value of serving the Lord and those he has put in our lives.

1. What are "heavenly treasures"? How does Luke 12:33-34 help you understand Matthew 6:19-21?

   _____

   _____

   _____

2. What material treasures or "wants" can you simply give up in an effort to open yourself more fully to the love of God?

   _____

   _____

   _____

3. What heavenly treasure do you particularly desire? What other heavenly treasures will you seek to store up?

   _____

   _____

   _____

When we consider the circumstances of those who heard Jesus' words, it may strike us as strange and unrealistic that Jesus told them not to worry about tomorrow. After all, they were poor, oppressed people. They likely had good reason to be anxious about food and clothing. Nevertheless, Jesus challenged them to "strive first for the kingdom of God and his righteousness, and all these things will be given to you as well" (Matthew 6:33). Some of them may have dismissed his words as impractical optimism.

Yet Jesus spoke lovingly and sincerely, backing up his challenge to trust God with logic: if God fed the birds and clothed the fields (see Matthew 6:26-30), would he not care for his children whom he dearly loved? On this premise, Jesus dedicated his entire life to doing God's will, and he calls us to do the same.

Clearly, Jesus made a promise that he expected his followers to rely on. Many Christians have done so, throwing in their lot completely with Christ. One such believer was Dietrich Bonhoeffer, a Lutheran pastor who lived in Hitler's Germany. He wrote, "'Be not anxious for the morrow. . . .' [This] is the gospel of Jesus Christ, and only so can it be understood. Only those who follow him and know him can receive this word as a promise of the love of his Father and as a deliverance from the thraldom of material things" (*The Cost of Discipleship*).

Treasuring the care that God had for him above his own safety and material well-being, Bonhoeffer resisted Nazi oppression and was executed in 1945.

1. Note all the verbs used in Matthew 6:24-34 to describe our orientation toward self or toward God. Which set of verbs speak most strongly to you? Why?

_____

_____

_____

2. How much of your day is filled with a persistent longing to acquire some new thing or have some new experience? How much of your day is spent listening to the Lord and what he desires for you? What steps can you take to stay better focused on the Lord's desires?

_____

_____

_____

3. Spend some time praying about your material possessions. Are there any you think the Lord is calling you to give away? What material goods might he want you to stop striving for? In what way or aspect of life will you try to rely on God's providence?

_____

_____

_____

Matthew 7:1-6: Freedom from the Tyranny of Judging Others

When we read admonitions like "Do not judge" and "Why do you see the speck in your neighbor's eye, but do not notice the log in your own eye?" (Matthew 7:1, 3), we must remember that Jesus spoke them to men and women like us, people eager to share his life and experience the fulfillment of his promises. And just as he challenged their hearts with his words, so too does he challenge ours.

In this passage, Jesus teaches us a new way of life, founded on faith in an all-loving, all-merciful Father. Grounded in this faith, our hearts treasure God's thoughts and ways above our own, and we learn to see ourselves and those around us with new eyes—eyes of love and mercy. Jesus illuminates the hypocrisy of our judgments of others and liberates us from self-deception. Through honest self-appraisal and humble self-knowledge, we can take the "log" out of our own eye (Matthew 7:5) and take a step toward freedom from the tyranny of judging others. As we come to have a godly perception of ourselves and our own faults, we can begin to love others with greater mercy and compassion.

In freedom, we become brothers and sisters to those around us. In the kingdom of God, a continual outpouring of grace enables us to live as Jesus commands us. As we allow the Holy Spirit to search our hearts and heal us, we can be confident that he will teach us how to love and how to put judgment of others behind us. Great joy and peace attend this new way of life.

1. Who was Jesus referring to in Matthew 7:5 when he said, "You hypocrite"? What does a hypocrite do?

_____

_____

_____

2. Who in your life are you especially critical of? What would it take for you to simply accept this person's eccentricities or failings and love him or her, rather than to continually judge?

_____

_____

_____

3. How would a constant awareness of our own faults help us to refrain from judging others? How would an awareness that we are judging one of God's beloved children aid in this effort? What can you do to cultivate such an awareness?

_____

_____

_____

Matthew 7:7-12: Prayer According to God's Will

Have you ever prayed for something and then been disappointed because God didn't answer your prayer the way you wanted? This is a common experience for most Christians, and as a result, we tend to question Jesus' promise that we shall receive if we but ask. But God *does* want to give us what we ask for—all that will help us to know his life and his love.

We must learn to pray according to God's will for us. Such prayer requires self-examination. Do we pray for selfish gain or to know God and his love? Or, more subtly, do we pray for what we think will most benefit self, neighbor, community, and world? Or do we pray that God's will be done with us as his obedient children in Christ? As we grow in Christian maturity through prayer, we become more and more at one with God's mind. We find that his desires for us become our desires. A life of prayer brings us ever more deeply into the heart and mind of God.

We turn to Jesus—who spent his life in prayer—as our model for a robust prayer life. When the time for his passion came, he asked the Father if the divine plan could be changed. But because Jesus had set his whole heart, his whole life, on doing the will of the Father, which at that moment had our awesome salvation at stake, Jesus completely submitted himself. "My Father, if it is possible, let this cup pass from me; yet not what I want but what you want. . . . My Father, if this cannot pass unless I drink it, your will be done" (Matthew 26:39, 42). As Jesus agonized in prayer about the upcoming events, the Holy Spirit conformed his will to the Father's perfect plan. He accepted the cross willingly.

1. The Golden Rule (see Matthew 7:12) immediately follows the passage about asking, searching, and knocking (see 7:7-11). Why do you suppose Matthew placed these verses in this order?

   _____

   _____

   _____

2. What would it cost you to pray that God's will be done rather than your own? What would you gain?

   _____

   _____

   _____

3. Do you currently have a prayer intention that you don't feel is being answered? If so, ask God for the grace to lovingly trust in his plan for you and your loved ones. If you still struggle, ask others to pray with you for peace.

   _____

   _____

   _____

Matthew 7:13-20: Bearing Good Fruit for the Kingdom

Twice in these verses, Jesus said, "You will know them by their fruits" (Matthew 7:16, 20). The word "fruit," from the Greek word *karpos*, means more than just an end product, the inevitable outcome of growth. The Greek word carries an implication of the *necessity* or *obligation* to bear fruit. All creation testifies to the *karpos*, to God's superabundant life expressed in fruit-bearing: buds become flowers; trees produce leaves; animals bear their young. Day after day, season after season, nature gives witness to the cooperation with God that bears fruit for his glory.

A true conversion to Jesus Christ presupposes a changed life—new habits, new sentiments, and new fruit borne from the vine grafted into Christ. And the good vine always bears good fruit. But a desire to be fruitful does not by itself produce good fruit. Often we tell ourselves that we want to bear good fruit, but in truth we actually resist oneness with Christ. Jesus said, "I am the vine, you are the branches. Those who abide in me and I in them bear much fruit, because apart from me you can do nothing" (John 15:5).

Of all created beings, humans alone can choose, by our free will, to bear good or evil fruit, to be a channel of God's life or a channel of decay and death. We make the ultimate choice, and it is a personal one. God the Father never ceases wanting us to be branches of the vine. And Jesus, our redeemer, now seated at the right hand of the throne of God, ceaselessly intercedes for us. He pours out his grace for us that we might choose his life. And he says to us, "My Father is glorified by this, that you bear much fruit and become my disciples" (John 15:8).

1. How do you tell good fruit from bad fruit in a grocery store? In contemporary culture, how do you tell the difference between true prophets and false prophets?

   _____

   _____

   _____

2. Why do you suppose the "road is hard that leads to life" (Matthew 7:14)? How does this relate to Matthew 11:30—"For my yoke is easy and my burden is light"? What is difficult, and what is easy?

   _____

   _____

   _____

3. What are the fruits of your life of faith? What could you do to bear even more fruit for your heavenly Father?

   _____

   _____

   _____

Matthew 7:21-29: Acting upon the Father's Will

Jesus concluded his Sermon on the Mount with the parable of the wise man and the fool. The parable presents us with a choice: to hear God's word and act upon it, or to hear God's word and reject it for worldly wisdom. Either way, God demands a response from us. Which choice will we make in our lives, and why will we choose it?

The psalmist chose to base his life on the Lord as his rock, knowing that the Lord's love endures forever (Psalm 118:1). With the Lord as his refuge, he proclaimed, "The LORD is my strength and my might; / he has become my salvation" (118:14). The prophet Isaiah made the same choice: "Trust in the LORD forever, / for in the LORD GOD / you have an everlasting rock" (26:4).

God's love stands as a rock, an immovable foundation of security and protection. He made this unfailing love known to us through Jesus Christ, who enables us to build our foundation on him. But to receive the fullness of his offer—peace and joy and love—we must respond with faith. "Those of steadfast mind you keep in peace—/ in peace because they trust in you" (Isaiah 26:3).

Blessed Mother Teresa of Calcutta urged us to accept God's love:

Let's believe in God's love and let's be faithful to him. If you look at the cross, you shall see his head lowered to kiss you. You will see his arms stretched out to embrace you. You will see his heart open to welcome you. Don't be afraid. He loves us, and he wants us to love one another. He loves us in spite of how poor and sinful we are. His love is true and we should believe in his love. (*One Heart Full of Love*)

1. What is the difference between saying "Lord, Lord" and doing "the will of [Jesus'] Father in heaven" (Matthew 7:21)?

_____

_____

_____

2. How can you make God the foundation of your life? How do you think this would help you to be able to hear his word and act upon it?

_____

_____

_____

3. When have you felt that God's love for you was as solid and unshakable as a rock? What would strengthen your belief that God loves you in spite of your weaknesses and sins?

_____

_____

_____

Matthew 8:1-4: Jesus' Healing Works

As we read through the Gospel of Matthew, we come to see the twofold nature of Jesus' mission—his "words" and his "works." In Matthew, chapters 5–7, Jesus spoke on the mountain as the new Moses, revealing the fulfillment of the law and the prophets. He spoke with authority and astonished his listeners with his teaching. In chapters 8–10, he traveled to Capernaum to perform works among the people of Galilee.

In this passage, Jesus revealed the power and love of God by healing the leper, the first miracle in a series of ten (Matthew 8:1–9:34). Jesus performed all these miracles as signs testifying to the reality of the kingdom of God. He also showed his power over the forces of evil, and he offered new life to all who opened their hearts to him. To these, he both revealed who he was and invited them to follow him. "Jesus . . . revealed his glory; and his disciples believed in him" (John 2:11).

By reflecting on Jesus' words and works, we grow stronger in faith. God the Father wants us to come to deeper intimacy with his Son, regardless of the level of our intellectual understanding. After all, the love of God "surpasses knowledge" (Ephesians 3:19) and is made possible only through the indwelling Spirit.

God wants us to approach Jesus as the leper did: "There was a leper who came to him and knelt before him, saying, 'Lord, if you choose, you can make me clean.' He stretched out his hand and touched him, saying, 'I do choose. Be made clean'" (Matthew 8:2-3).

1. Jesus used the word "clean" (Matthew 8:3). What are some synonyms and antonyms for "clean"?

_____

_____

_____

2. The leper knew that Jesus could either choose to heal him or not, but the leper left the choice up to Jesus. How similar is this interaction to your prayer life with Jesus?

_____

_____

_____

3. What emotional, physical, or spiritual request for healing do you have for Jesus? How can you approach Jesus with your request? How can you willingly leave it in Jesus' hands?

_____

_____

_____

Matthew 8:5-13: The Authority of Jesus

The centurion understood authority. He had soldiers under his authority and was himself answerable to authority above him (see Matthew 8:9). He respected and obeyed the legitimate authority over him, and he received respect and obedience from those under his authority. This understanding opened the centurion to great faith in Jesus. The centurion knew that Jesus could heal his servant—even at a great distance. He knew that Jesus had only to "speak the word" (8:8), and his servant would be healed.

How do we understand the authority of God? We know that God created the world and gave us dominion over it (see Genesis 1:26). We know that the Father has given Jesus "all authority in heaven and on earth" (Matthew 28:18) and has placed him at the head of the church (Colossians 1:18). We know, therefore, that all authority in heaven and on earth ultimately derives from God.

When we recognize, respect, and obey God's perfect authority, we grow in a desire to comply with the laws he has given us through the church. When we keep these laws, the result is that we lead more loving and fruitful lives. We bear witness to the gifts that spring from God's authority.

Like the centurion, our acknowledgment of God's authority opens us to great faith. When we pray in the name of Jesus, we invoke his authority over all things, including fear, sickness, anxiety, and sin. Although we are "not worthy" (Matthew 8:8), Jesus rejoices at our faith, calms our fears and anxieties, makes us well, and removes our sin.

1. How does the centurion's understanding of authority add to your understanding of Jesus' authority? How does it add to your understanding of faith in Jesus?

_____

_____

_____

2. Why are the laws of the church a gift to us? Why do you think a grateful attitude toward God's authority, as manifested in the church, would help us to bear fruit in our lives?

_____

_____

_____

3. How often do you pray in the name of Jesus and invoke his authority over fear, sickness, or sin? How would your faith grow from doing so?

_____

_____

_____

Matthew 8:14-17: The Fullness of Jesus' Healing

We all know the feeling of waking up in the morning and dreading the day's events. Perhaps we dread some task scheduled to happen that day, or we face another day of chronic pain or another day caring for a sick and cranky child. Like Peter's mother-in-law, bedridden and feverish, we know the physical, emotional, and spiritual burdens of the day. During these times of infirmity, we easily become depressed, making it almost impossible for us to love and care for others.

When Jesus heard about Peter's mother-in-law, he took her by the hand and healed her. The fever immediately left her, and she began to serve Jesus and his disciples. What power, authority, and love Jesus' presence manifests! Nothing in life—no illness, no negative emotion, no sin, no demon—can stand against him.

Matthew tells us this story to show how Jesus exercises his authority through love. Jesus loves us so much that he became a man, entered our weak and wounded condition, and triumphed over it by giving up his own life on the cross. He now invites us to receive his love and healing power: "He heals the brokenhearted, / and binds up their wounds" (Psalm 147:3).

When we believe in Jesus, partake of his mysteries at the altar, and keep his commandments, the Spirit enters into us more deeply and gives us the power to reflect Jesus' love more fully. Jesus wants to rule our activities through his Spirit, moving us to love the Lord and to serve his people with humility and compassion (see *Catechism of the Catholic Church*, 2084). Strengthened by the presence of the Spirit in us, let us walk in the authority and compassion of Jesus.

1. Imagine people crowded around Jesus, hoping for cures for their wide range of illnesses. How would you describe their attitudes and expectations?

   _____

   _____

   _____

2. What physical, emotional, or spiritual wounds might you bring to Jesus for healing? What might hold you back from asking him to heal you?

   _____

   _____

   _____

3. How can you better reflect Christ's healing presence to others?

   _____

   _____

   _____

Matthew 8:18-22: The Costs of Discipleship

The first would-be disciple, a scribe who professed himself willing to forsake all to follow Jesus, acted impulsively. Jesus saw the condition of his heart and knew that his initial fervor would soon fizzle. He therefore suggested to the man just what his commitment might entail (see Matthew 8:19-20). The second disciple, who seemed willing to follow Jesus but had pressing family matters to attend to, indicated that Jesus' call to discipleship was not his highest priority. Jesus urged him not to allow worldly concerns to cloud his perceptions of the kingdom of God. Only by putting God's will first would he insure his family's well-being (see 8:21-22).

As Jesus began to reveal his identity, he used the title "Son of Man" (Matthew 8:20). On the one hand, this title, used about seventy times in the gospels, means "man" or son of Adam and emphasizes humanity's smallness before God (see Psalm 8:5). On the other hand, "Son of Man" describes an eternal king that all nations will serve, a heavenly savior. In Jewish apocalyptic writings, the title described a person endowed with glorious power, one who would come at the end of time to rule the kingdom of God (see Daniel 7:13-14).

In these short dialogues, Jesus gave us a veiled reference to his identity. Only those with ears to hear will recognize him as the long-awaited Messiah. As disciples of Christ, do we recognize Jesus as the Lord of our lives? It can be challenging to follow Jesus, but the blessings we receive as we take each step will overshadow any struggle we encounter along the way!

1. What does this passage reveal about Jesus' understanding of himself and his mission?

_____

_____

_____

2. In what ways do you relate with the fully human Jesus? In what ways do you relate with the divine Son of Man?

_____

_____

_____

3. What aspects of your life are "dead"? How can you let go of these "dead" things to free yourself to become a disciple of Christ?

_____

_____

_____

Matthew 8:23-27: Faith in Times of Crisis

Jesus' calming of the storm continues the flow of miracle stories begun earlier with the healing of a leper (see Matthew 8:1-17). The storm episode intensified the disciples' wonder at Jesus' authority: "What sort of man is this, that even the winds and the sea obey him?" (8:27). All together, these events dramatically reveal Jesus to be the Messiah who inaugurates the kingdom of God.

Immediately after the scene in which Jesus emphasized the dedication required to follow him (see Matthew 8:18-22), the "disciples followed" Jesus into the boat (8:23). By following him, they were trying to live as genuine disciples. When the wind rose and the waves began swamping the boat, however, fear overcame them, and their faith evaporated.

Matthew used the Greek word *seismos* to describe the storm (see Matthew 8:24). Elsewhere in Matthew (and in the New Testament), this word describes the upheaval and calamity that will occur in the end times, when tribulation will shake the church (see 24:7; Mark 13:8). Use of this word for the storm helped early Christian readers to realize that they must not let themselves be immobilized by persecution and adversity.

Like the early Christians, when we are seized with fear, we have a choice: we can let the fear overwhelm us, or we can place our trust in Jesus. The good news is that as we experience the saving power of Christ, our faith comes to life. We know we can depend on Jesus—no matter what is happening around us.

1. The disciples were clearly afraid of dying (see Matthew 8:25). Why did this upset Jesus so much?

_____

_____

_____

2. How can you pray with confidence when you call out to God for help? Instead of crying out "Lord, save us" in times of crisis, what do you suppose you could say?

_____

_____

_____

3. How do you wish to react next time you find yourself in a crisis situation? What role will Jesus play?

_____

_____

_____

Matthew 8:28-34: Allowing Jesus to Heal Us

Gadara was a city east of the Jordan River in the non-Jewish region of the Decapolis. Even here, in pagan territory, Jesus demonstrated his awesome power and authority. The demons recognized and feared Jesus' power (see Matthew 8:29), and they mistakenly believed they could escape torment or worse, death, by possessing the nearby herd of swine (see 8:31).

When the townspeople came out to see Jesus, we might expect that Jesus' great miracle would heal their unbelief. Instead, they became fearful of Jesus and "begged him to leave their neighborhood" (Matthew 8:34). Doesn't this puzzle us? Yet God has shown us his power and love many times, and we have responded to his invitations for serious conversion by turning our hearts away.

God wants us to experience cleansing and freedom from sins such as self-centeredness, anger, deception, and lust. Through his love, Jesus shines light on our lives and shows us more clearly the need to change these habits and attitudes and be healed. As our eyes open to these truths, we either decide to allow Jesus to make us whole, or we resist his work.

Fear is the single most important factor that causes us to turn our hearts away from God; fear paralyzes us. We so enjoy the comfort of our lives, with all our sins and problems, that we forget God's desire that we become one with him in Jesus Christ. Through Jesus' death on the cross, he releases us from fear. Let us listen and respond positively to this great truth.

1. Many who met or saw Jesus did not fear him. What do you think the townspeople saw that frightened them? What does this imply about the townspeople?

   _____

   _____

   _____

2. What fears separate you from the love of Christ? Pray earnestly and often for Christ's healing of these fears.

   _____

   _____

   _____

3. What courage did Jesus show in this passage? How can you emulate Jesus' courage?

   _____

   _____

   _____

Matthew 9:1-8: Signs of the Kingdom

With ten miracle stories in just two chapters (see Matthew 8:1–9:34), we may be surprised to learn that Jesus' ability to perform miracles was *not* Matthew's main concern. Instead, Matthew strove to affirm and articulate Jesus' role as the Messiah who had come to free the world of sin and darkness through his cross and to usher in the kingdom of God.

Matthew's story of the paralyzed man does just that. This man experienced two kinds of healing—physical and spiritual. Both signaled the coming kingdom, in which the Son of Man would complete his work of healing and restoration. In the paralyzed man's case, Jesus confirms his power and authority to forgive sins with his ability to heal and restore.

Such miraculous healings show that God's power can transform us, even on the physical level. Some people try to discredit healing stories in the Bible because they don't believe in a connection between physical healing and spiritual forces, either good or evil. Most of us do not attribute *all* sickness to the work of demons or *all* healing to the miraculous work of God. However, doctors continue to find that prayer can positively impact our ability to heal.

The crowd was amazed at the healing of the paralyzed man because God had given such authority to human beings! Matthew would have us ponder this truth (as he and the early community of believers undoubtedly had done) and have us consider it in light of all that Jesus, as the Messiah of word and deed, has done. Truly, we should take Jesus seriously.

1. How does this passage add to your understanding of Jesus? How does it add to your understanding of Christians in general?

_____

_____

_____

2. Do you accept Jesus' authority to forgive your sins and heal you? What attitudes might prevent you from fully accepting this truth?

_____

_____

_____

3. What spiritual paralysis can you identify within yourself? Bring it to Jesus, and ask for healing.

_____

_____

_____

Matthew 9:9-13: Responding to Jesus' Call

Matthew was an outcast—a Jew who served the financial arm of the Roman Empire. He probably felt that in many ways he had betrayed his own people by making accommodations with a pagan culture. He no doubt endured scornful looks and bitter words from all those who disdained his livelihood. And Matthew almost surely followed a common practice of tax collectors: overcharging his clients to make extra money for himself (see Luke 3:12-13). Matthew knew sin. He knew he needed salvation. When Jesus called, Matthew followed (Matthew 9:9).

Imagine Matthew's hope and joy when he heard Jesus say, "Those who are well have no need of a physician, but those who are sick. . . . For I have come to call not the righteous but sinners" (Matthew 9:12, 13). This teaching in particular must have strongly influenced Matthew, as it does all of us who have a need for such a physician. The wonder of all wonders is that God calls us while we are still sinners (see Romans 5:8)!

The popular, secular opinion of human nature states that we are all basically good people. When we step back from our wishful thinking, however, we must more honestly admit that we have all been wounded by original sin (see Romans 3:10-12, 23). We have all sought after our own needs and desires before thinking about the desires of the Lord (see 7:15, 17-20). When Matthew realized this, he forsook his cherished possessions and ideas and followed Jesus. The same can also be true for us. If we ask him, the Holy Spirit will not only show us our sin, but he will also speak words of comfort and hope to us, calling us to Jesus, our great healer.

1. Why did the Pharisees ask, "Why does your teacher eat with tax collectors and sinners?" (Matthew 9:11)? How do you imagine they reacted when Jesus said, "Go and learn what this means, 'I desire mercy, not sacrifice'" (9:13)?

_____

_____

_____

2. Why do you think we are so tempted to think of our own needs and desires before those of God? Of others?

_____

_____

_____

3. How do you, personally, respond to Jesus' call to sinners? How can more frequent reception of the Sacrament of Reconciliation help you to be convicted of and repent of your sins?

_____

_____

_____

Matthew 9:14-17: Christ Brings Renewal

Through Jesus, the old order was passing away, and the new order was beginning. Jesus described this new order, this new way of relating to God, using various similes. He likened it to a wedding feast in which the guests rejoice in the bridegroom's presence (see Matthew 9:15). Jesus, the bridegroom, fulfilled the Old Testament prophecies that said God would forgive and join himself to his children as through a marriage covenant (see Hosea 2:18-20; Isaiah 62:4-5).

The parables of the wineskins and the patched cloth illustrate the newness of all that was happening. Jesus creates things anew; he doesn't merely patch them up. New wine signifies the new era: Jesus dispenses the new wine for us, the new creation in Christ. He came, in fact, to renew the whole universe through his birth, death, and resurrection.

The body of Christ reflects the new order established by Christ. It shines with the love, harmony, peace, and unity that come from Christ—for the whole world to see. Jesus wants his body on earth to mirror the love and unity he shares with his Father and the Holy Spirit. Sadly, however, we still see disharmony and disunity within and between the Christian churches.

As Christians, we should take seriously our responsibility to pray for and work toward unity within and among Christian churches, according to the mind and heart of Christ. Disunity and division in our own time prevent the fulfillment of this new reality in Christ. The bridegroom cannot fully rejoice while division exists among the very people he came to gather together.

1. How would you describe the setting and atmosphere of this passage? In what ways does reflecting on the setting help you to understand the meaning of the passage?

2. Do you have faith that you can be renewed in Christ each day? What could you do to better reflect Christ's peace, joy, and love?

3. What is one practical action step you can take to help overcome divisions between your church and other churches in your community?

Matthew 9:18-26: Toward a Deeper Faith

In these two stories, Matthew described the peoples' responses to Jesus. One man, a leader of the synagogue, fell at Jesus' feet and begged him to heal his daughter. Another woman, who had suffered from chronic hemorrhaging, fell at Jesus' feet and confessed that she was healed by simply touching the hem of his garment. But others, those from the synagogue leader's household, showed no faith in Jesus. They mocked him and laughed at him as he went about healing the leader's daughter.

What is our response to Jesus? When we act out of envy or bitterness, does this not signify a lack of faith? Are we not each saying, "I have a right to be angry because nobody (not even God) is looking after my interests"? When we repent of a specific sin but know that we will probably go ahead and commit it again, is this not a lack of faith in the power of the blood to cleanse and free us from sin? When we become restless during Scripture reading or prayer time, is it because we don't expect Jesus to speak to us and give us peace and joy in his presence? What then do these actions say about who we believe Jesus to be? Do we view him as a moral leader, a wonder-working healer, a holy man, or the eternal Son of God, our perfect and complete salvation?

Our unbelief manifests itself in many ways. Jesus wants us to put aside negative thoughts and actions and replace them with faith like the ruler's and the hemorrhaging woman's. He wants to tell us, "Do not fear, only believe" (Mark 5:36). He can say this only if we try to put off our old attitudes and mind-sets and ask him to give us a new mind formed in his image.

1. How did Jesus respond to the laughter in the leader's household? Who do you suppose moved the crowd outside? Why was that important?

_____

_____

_____

2. Why do you suppose it is so much easier to mock and laugh at Jesus than believe in him? How would you further characterize these two responses to Jesus?

_____

_____

_____

3. How does unbelief manifest itself in your life? How can you renew your mind in Christ's image?

_____

_____

_____

Matthew 9:27-31: Faith as Intelligent Adherence

The prophet Isaiah had told of a time when, out of the gloom and darkness, the eyes of the blind would see (see Isaiah 29:18). This prophecy characterizes much of ancient Israel's messianic literature. When John the Baptist sent his disciples to ask Jesus if he was the Messiah, Jesus said, "Go and tell John what you hear and see: the blind receive their sight, the lame walk, the lepers are cleansed, the deaf hear, the dead are raised, and the poor have the good news brought to them" (Matthew 11:4-5).

Jesus is the Messiah, the one spoken of in the Old Testament, whom God sent to save his people. When the two blind men cried out to Jesus to have mercy on them, Jesus asked if they believed that he could heal them (see Matthew 9:28). The Greek word Matthew used for "believe" was *pistis*, which means "faith." This faith comes from intelligent adherence, not from a blind leap in the dark.

For the blind men, having *pistis* would have involved knowing the prophecies about the coming Messiah and being able to measure Jesus' words and deeds against these predictions. In other words, Jesus was asking the men if they believed that he was the Messiah, the Son of God. Their physical healing came about as a result of their act of faith (see Matthew 9:29).

For the sake of our faith, Jesus fulfilled all the Old Testament prophecies concerning the coming Messiah. We should look at the Old Testament evidence and compare it to what we know about Jesus. When we do, we can then ask for a believer's faith. The extent to which we can say "I believe" is the extent to which we experience God's love and power in our lives.

1. What do you think the phrase "And their eyes were opened" (Matthew 9:30) means? (See also John 9:10-11; Acts 28:27; Ephesians 1:18.)

   _____

   _____

   _____

2. Often we are most blind to our own faults. What do you imagine you might see if you asked Jesus to heal you of your blindness?

   _____

   _____

   _____

3. Do you *know* you have faith? Find at least one way in which you know you have faith in Jesus. Hold that knowledge close to your heart.

   _____

   _____

   _____

Matthew 9:32-38: Jesus, the Compassionate Shepherd

Jesus saw that the crowds were subject to the whims of their passions and desires. Many were crippled by fear, unbelief, and the lies of Satan. Despite all this, Jesus looked on them with compassion (see Matthew 9:36). As a reflection of the Father's love, Jesus went about "proclaiming the good news of the kingdom, and curing every disease and every sickness" (9:35).

With the healing of the demoniac, Jesus gave another sign that he wants to heal us all, so that we might share in the life of the Father. He wants to show us the ways in which our bondage to sin keeps us from witnessing God's glory in our lives. The Pharisees saw Jesus' deeds, but they insisted that he acted in league with the devil (see Matthew 9:34). Ignoring this attack, Jesus continued his mission and invited his disciples to go out as laborers into the harvest (see 9:37-38).

In the words of Blessed Mother Teresa of Calcutta, "Jesus did not stop his works of charity because the Pharisees and others hated him or tried to spoil His Father's work. He just went about doing good" (*Total Surrender*). We, too, embracing Jesus as the Messiah, work together as the body of Christ to announce the good news and to lead others to the salvation Jesus offers us.

In the kingdom of God, Jesus reigns as Lord and King. Those of us who embrace the kingdom know who we are and we know our King. We have confidence in our King's love for us, all of us. He is our consolation (see 2 Corinthians 1:3-4) and our strength (see Psalm 28:7-8). As a result, we are driven by a new desire to love and serve God.

1. What was Jesus talking about when he referred to the "plentiful harvest" and the "laborers" (see Matthew 9:37)? Where today do you find that plentiful harvest? Where do you see the laborers?

_____

_____

_____

2. How does your desire to build God's kingdom on earth spur you on to love and serve the Lord? What do you think would give you an even greater desire to serve God?

_____

_____

_____

3. How can Christians avoid discouragement and paralysis when they encounter resistance and persecution in serving the Lord?

_____

_____

_____

Matthew 10:1-7: Commissioning the Apostles to Preach

The apostles had traveled with Jesus around the Galilean countryside as he proclaimed the good news of the kingdom, curing every disease and sickness (see Matthew 9:35). Then Jesus sent them out as his ambassadors to gain firsthand experience as missionaries. With this commission, he empowered them to heal as he had healed, to cast out demons as he had cast them out, and to proclaim, as he had, that the kingdom of God has come near (see 10:1, 7).

Jesus chose these quite ordinary men who had little of what our world deems necessary for success—education, wealth, social standing—to carry on his work. These are the same men who later gathered in prayer after Jesus' ascension and who, after the coming of the Holy Spirit at Pentecost, preached and baptized so that three thousand were added to their number (see Acts 2:41). They remained faithful to their calling, for "every day in the temple and at home they did not cease to teach and proclaim Jesus as the Messiah," despite the persecutions they endured (5:42).

By our baptism, we, too, receive Jesus' commission to follow in his footsteps and to preach the message of salvation. The Holy Spirit empowers us, like the apostles, to proclaim this good news of Jesus Christ. If we are faithful to our calling as ministers of Christ's word, the gospel *will* spread, and God's kingdom *will* grow. This passage also brings the role of the clergy to the forefront. We pray that they deeply know Jesus' truth and power, manifest it in their ministry, and remain ever faithful to their responsibility to proclaim the gospel message. Let us pray also that we may faithfully and generously do our part in carrying out the mission of Jesus.

1. What is the connection between the nearness of the kingdom of heaven and healing?

_____

_____

_____

2. Why do you think Jesus limited the apostles' first mission to "the lost sheep of the house of Israel" (Matthew 10:5-6)?

_____

_____

_____

3. Do you envision your name on the ever-growing list of Jesus' disciples? Why or why not? In what way do you go out into the world—to all nations—to proclaim the good news?

_____

_____

_____

Matthew 10:8-15: Reliance on God

Matthew's gospel presented not only historical events but also theological interpretations of historical events. In doing so, Matthew provided guidance to future Christian communities that would respond to the call of discipleship. He clearly stated that the great commission applied to *all* future believers: "Go therefore and make disciples of all nations" (Matthew 28:19).

To preach the good news, the disciple of Christ must first have confidence in the power of the gospel to change lives—to heal and to purify (see Matthew 10:8). Second, the disciple of Christ must have a sense of urgency about pursuing the mission. He or she does not delay or even wait for the "proper equipment" (10:9-10). Third, the disciple of Christ does not expect material gain or profit—preaching the gospel is not strictly business; it is personal.

Jesus taught the apostles to rely solely on God's goodness and generosity. Such an attitude recognizes God as a loving Father who faithfully provides for his people and never abandons them. And when the world rejects the disciple of Christ, the proper response is not condemnation or retribution but a symbolic shaking of the dust from their feet (see Matthew 10:14).

Many of us do not think this way—we think about ourselves first; we rely on ourselves. We often act as though God were miserly, begrudging of his love, not really caring for us. This mind-set affects and limits the power of the gospel message we preach. We have a missionary's heart when we trust in God and have confidence in his generosity and faithfulness.

1. Why do you suppose it was important that the disciples not bring any money, clothes, or bags with them? What might it mean to you to "travel light" in order to take up Jesus' call to mission?

_____

_____

_____

2. What does this passage teach you about what you have to offer as a missionary of Christ? Have you ever encountered rejection for speaking God's word? If so, what did you learn through that experience?

_____

_____

_____

3. What are some ways you could more actively bring God's presence or word into your home? Your parish? Your workplace?

_____

_____

_____

Matthew 10:16-23: Guidance for Coming Persecution

Jesus knew that the primitive church would experience widespread persecution as it proclaimed the good news throughout the world. Despite this, he told his apostles to go out "like sheep into the midst of wolves" (Matthew 10:16). He warned them of the great difficulties ahead—that even their own families would persecute them and, in some cases, condemn them to death (see 10:21).

But Jesus did not leave the disciples defenseless. He promised to send them the Holy Spirit, who would teach and guide them in every situation and help them to be "wise as serpents and innocent as doves" (Matthew 10:16). Like innocent doves, they would not judge or grow angry with the world. Like wise serpents, they would not fall into the traps set for them.

Sometimes we, too, may feel like sheep going out among wolves. We may face ridicule or rejection because of our beliefs. Worldly people may try to lure us into situations that reveal our weaknesses or test our faith. We may feel tempted to lash out at these "wolves" or to write them off. Or we may feel fearful and timid, reluctant to live and share our faith.

Our protection and wisdom come from the Holy Spirit as we seek God through prayer and from the grounding we gain by reading Scripture and hearing it proclaimed in the liturgy. With minds filled with the truth of God's word, we have the strength and knowledge to withstand those who oppose Christ and his way of life.

1. The advice on how to handle coming persecution was very applicable to Matthew's community, which was being persecuted. How applicable is it to you and your community? Why?

_____

_____

_____

2. What do you think is the surest way to gain wisdom and to preserve innocence in a world full of its own wisdom and ample opportunity to lose innocence?

_____

_____

_____

3. Recall a time when you experienced ridicule or rejection because of your faith. How did you respond? What is your defense against the "wolves" in the world?

_____

_____

_____

Matthew 10:24-33: Comfort and Strength in Christ

"It is enough for the disciple to be like the teacher" (Matthew 10:25). Jesus' call to his disciples was, and continues to be, first and foremost an invitation to become like him. When he called Andrew and Simon Peter and invited them to become fishers of people (see 4:19), he meant that by following him, they would be transformed into his likeness. His heart would become their heart. And like their master, they would actively proclaim the good news for all to hear.

Jesus also warned of the challenges and difficulties inherent in the life of a disciple: "If they have called the master of the house Beelzebul, how much more will they malign those of his household" (Matthew 10:25). At the same time, Jesus repeatedly encouraged them not to fear what might happen to them (see 10:26, 28, 31).

As members of Jesus' body, we all share in his victory over the evil one. Though Satan tempts us, we need never succumb, however fierce the attack or however weak we feel. Our master—the Lord Jesus Christ—resides within us as our comfort and strength. As we turn to him in humble faith, he pours out his wisdom and gives us all we need (see Matthew 10:19-20).

In today's society, our belief in God and obedience to his commands come under frequent fire. But we have hope and continue along the path of discipleship. Christ is in us, and his love surrounds us. He will never abandon us. He will acknowledge us before the Father as we remain faithful to him (see Matthew 10:32). Let us not lose heart, for he who is in us is greater than he who is in the world (see 1 John 4:4).

1. In your own words, who or what should we fear, and who or what should we not fear?

_____

_____

_____

2. How easily do you fall into a state of fear for things Jesus teaches that you need not fear? Why? How can you avoid this?

_____

_____

_____

3. How do you envision yourself walking through life filled with Christian courage? Describe what you see. What could you do to increase your confidence in God's care for you and make this vision more of a reality?

_____

_____

_____

Matthew 10:34–11:1: Taking Up the Cross

Christ calls us to witness to our new discipleship in him—to testify, both in word and deed, that Jesus has overcome sin and inaugurated the kingdom of God. This new life, he explains, manifests itself within us in a radical way. Jesus also said that divisions would occur as the light within us grows brighter and as it shines into the darkness.

As committed disciples, we bind our hearts and souls to the Lord, and we allow Christ's word, like a two-edged sword, to separate the light from the darkness within us. As the light within us begins to shine, the darkness gives way. This loving light of Christ far exceeds even our love for family, and we must put this love to work, however difficult that might be (see Matthew 10:37-38).

Dietrich Bonhoeffer, a German Lutheran pastor who was imprisoned and put to death by the Nazi regime, put it this way: "The peace of Jesus is the cross. But the cross is the sword God wields on earth. It creates division. The son against the father, the daughter against the mother, the member of the house against the head—all this will happen in the name of God's kingdom and his peace. That is the work which Christ performs on earth" (*The Cost of Discipleship*).

God's love radically differs from the love that humanity has for its own flesh and blood. God's love for man means the cross and the way of discipleship. That cross and that way are our life and our resurrection.

1. How do you think Jesus' hearers might have reacted to his teachings in this passage? Do you think they "got it"? Why or why not? How do you react?

_____

_____

_____

2. What has it cost you to "take up the cross" (Matthew 10:38)? Recall some concrete examples of how you have "lost" your life for Christ's sake (10:39). In what ways did you then experience "finding" it?

_____

_____

_____

3. How will you respond to loved ones who don't accept your commitment to Christ? Ask the Holy Spirit for grace and wisdom as you respond.

_____

_____

_____

Matthew 11:2-15: He Who Is to Come

We have all seen time-lapse photography that dramatically depicts what happens when downpours of rain flood an arid desert plain. Seeds germinate and an abundance of flowers, plants, and grains spring to life, radically changing the environment. Isaiah described a similar transformation with the appearance of the Messiah (see Isaiah 35:1-10). Just as the rains bring forth bountiful fruits from barren lands, so would the Messiah bring redemption and restoration to a needy world.

Jesus alluded to this passage from Isaiah when he told John the Baptist's emissaries to report back to him the signs and wonders they saw happening: "[T]he blind receive their sight, the lame walk, the lepers are cleansed, the deaf hear, the dead are raised, and the poor have good news brought to them" (Matthew 11:5). While not a direct claim to messiahship, Jesus' answer revealed the type of messiahship he brought forth—not wrathful judgment or political-military power, but healings and blessings.

We ask the same question John's disciples ask Jesus: "Are you the one who is to come?" (Matthew 11:3). As we read and reflect on Scripture and God's revelation to us, the answer becomes clearer and clearer to us. As we open our ears to hear (see 11:15), the Holy Spirit reveals to us that Jesus is indeed the one who is to come. And as we receive this life-giving truth into our hearts, our "soil" will absorb the moisture that brings healing, restoration, and abundant fruitfulness. How blessed we are when we recognize who Jesus truly is (see 11:6)!

1. What "way" did John the Baptist come to prepare (Matthew 11:10; see also 3:1-3)? Describe some of the ways in which John carried out his mission as herald of the Messiah (see Luke 3:7-18).

_____

_____

_____

2. Seeing Jesus as the Messiah most often begins with repentance. Explain how this has been true for you.

_____

_____

_____

3. What obstructs your efforts to open your ears and listen to the Holy Spirit's revelation and guidance? What methods of prayer and meditation are most effective for you?

_____

_____

_____

Matthew 11:16-19: Wisdom Justified by Deeds

We detect a note of patient weariness in the Lord's voice as he chided the crowd for its refusal to accept the truth. The unbelievers behaved like obstinate children, rejecting everything and anything offered them. How reminiscent of a parent coaxing a youngster to eat his or her greens!

Both John the Baptist and Jesus came to the Jews announcing what they, as a people, had longed for centuries to hear—the arrival of the Messiah, the Son of David, the King of Israel! Like sullen children, some of the Jews disdained John the Baptist and his message. When Jesus came, they rejected him as well, calling him a blasphemous companion of unsavory people.

How many times have we heard people reject the Christian message for petty or irrational reasons? "I don't need someone telling me what to do. If God is all love, how could he condemn me to hell?" We have all heard these and similar rationalizations; on occasion, we, too, may have used some of them as we struggled to be true to the gospel.

Matthew noted that history would be the judge of who is right and who is wrong: "Wisdom is vindicated by her deeds" (Matthew 11:19). Likewise, the words of the psalmist are as true today as they were in the time of Jesus' earthly ministry: "The wicked will not stand in the judgment" (Psalm 1:5). Yet God is faithful and merciful; he will never abandon those who turn to him. In Jesus, we have a loving intercessor at the right hand of the Father, constantly interceding for all who call upon his name.

1. What does Matthew 11:19 indicate about Jesus and his ministry (see also 9:10-13)? About what some people thought of him? Why do you think they were puzzled or offended by him?

_____

_____

_____

2. What kind of Messiah do you want Jesus to be? Do you accept Jesus as the Messiah he in fact is? If you have made your own "preferred" image of him, how can you let go of this?

_____

_____

_____

3. How does this passage affect your outlook on the importance of deeds? What deeds and whose deeds? What wisdom do your own deeds demonstrate? None? Self-reliance? Responsibility? Compassion? Worship of God alone? Love for your enemies?

_____

_____

_____

Matthew 11:20-24: Accepting Our Hope for Salvation

Jesus conducted much of his ministry in Bethsaida, Chorazin, and Capernaum, all towns in the region of Galilee. There he performed many healings and miracles, revealed the deepest meanings of the Scriptures, and told the people about God's love. These townspeople heard more of Jesus' teaching and saw more of his deeds than any other people across the Holy Land, yet they rejected him.

God expressed his mercy toward humanity through Jesus, who is one with the Father. God sent Jesus, the object of his love, to be our Lord and our brother, our Savior and our friend. God intends for us to walk with Jesus, to follow his lead. We often find this difficult, though. The difficulty stems from our tendency to resist Jesus, to marginalize him, and to not comprehend his centrality in God's plan of salvation.

Christ lives with us—and in us—always. He promises us, "I will not leave you orphaned" (John 14:18). With Christ in our lives, we may overcome our tendencies to doubt his identity and his intimate role in our salvation. Let us examine our daily decisions to see how they reflect our faith in Jesus. We may then remind ourselves throughout the day to act from a simple trust and confidence in Jesus.

We *can* change. If we ask in prayer, the Holy Spirit will show us Jesus' role in the Father's plan for our salvation. We can also read the Scriptures that reveal Jesus as Lord over all things (see Ephesians 1:3-10, 17-23; Philippians 2:5-11; Colossians 1:15-20; Revelation 1:5-8). He is the source of all wisdom, power, love, and faith.

1. In this passage, Jesus rebuked entire cities. What does this suggest to you about the importance of societal repentance and spiritual conversion?

_____

_____

_____

2. What are you and fellow Christians doing to bring the good news to your local community?

_____

_____

_____

3. What deeds of power has Jesus done in your life? Did they lead you to repentance in any areas of your life? How have these deeds impacted your faith?

_____

_____

_____

Matthew 11:25-27: A Childlike Openness to God

In Jesus' day, Jewish society viewed the Pharisees as moral and religious leaders—and for good reason. The Pharisees possessed many admirable qualities and exercised great discipline in adhering to the law. The common people respected and honored them for this. Perhaps Jesus tried so hard to reach the Pharisees for these reasons.

But something in the Pharisees' temperaments predisposed many of them to reject Jesus' teachings. Their elevated status in society might have had something to do with it, since Jesus came from a lower class. More specifically, however, the Pharisees lacked those qualities that Jesus said were needed to enter into God's kingdom: a humble, childlike spirit and dependence on God, rather than self.

Jesus praised the Father for revealing the hidden things of salvation to those like "infants" (Matthew 11:25). The "wise and intelligent," on the other hand, dismissed both his miracles and his message. This passage highlights an important theme of Matthew's gospel: "Unless you change and become like children, you will never enter the kingdom of heaven" (18:3).

The Pharisees had no monopoly on self-righteous thinking; we all tend to indulge in it. To stay in step with God's Spirit, however, we must constantly try to nurture a teachable spirit within ourselves. Are we closed to the Spirit's voice in Scripture or in the authentic teaching of the church? If we open our hearts, the Father can reveal to us his truth—and the things that keep us from being his children, as well.

1. Why, in your opinion, is God's truth "hidden" from the wise and intelligent (Matthew 11:25)? What does verse 27 reveal about Jesus' self-understanding and his knowledge of his role in God's plan for salvation?

2. What childlike qualities do you see in yourself? How do they help you understand God and his revealed truth?

3. Do you recognize any ways in which your natural intelligence has been an obstacle in your relationship with God? If so, what could you do to remedy this?

Matthew 11:28-30: Peace in the Life of Christ

Rejected by his own people, Jesus extended his great invitation to all persons of every nation, race, and generation. He wants all people to come to him and learn from him how to live. He wants to give us all a vision that enables us to love God and set our sights on his heavenly kingdom.

On life's journey, we often tire and weaken from the cares and trials that we face; life can seem so burdensome and oppressive! Occasionally we are our own undoing, making choices that lead us away from God. At other times, we are faced with illnesses and other troubles we have not brought upon ourselves. Whatever the case, Jesus invites us to yoke ourselves to him and to learn from him.

Once we accept the yoke of Christ, we will experience the peace that comes only from the Prince of Peace. Once united with Jesus, we will learn how to choose not ways that lead to exhaustion or oppression but his way. Just as Jesus yielded his life and will to the Father and was one with him, Jesus asks us to become one with him and assures us that we will then know the unity and the peace that come from God alone.

Jesus refreshes us; he gives us life. He eases our burdens and lessens our sufferings. The healing and deliverance we experience in Jesus signal the forthcoming fullness of salvation. Seeing our lives through this prism of God's love rouses in us a renewed desire to be further united with him—to be further conformed to him. This is the light yoke of Christ.

1. What is your understanding of Jesus' words that his yoke is easy and his burden light?

   _____

   _____

   _____

2. In what ways do you feel "heavy laden"? Ask God to help you let go of these burdens and give them over to him now.

   _____

   _____

   _____

3. What do you think Christ wants you to learn from him as you take up his yoke? How does Christ's yoke give you "rest"?

   _____

   _____

   _____

Matthew 12:1-8: The Primacy of Mercy

The law of Moses included numerous rites, such as ritual bathing and sacrificial offerings, all of which were external actions meant to justify the people before God. Somewhat in contrast, mercy suggests an internal orientation that requires a selfless, self-giving attitude. The Greek word for "mercy" used here is *eleos*, connoting compassion for the sufferings of others.

When Jesus quoted from Hosea 6:6, saying, "I desire mercy and not sacrifice" (Matthew 12:7), he highlighted the difference between internal and external devotion to God. Throughout his ministry, Jesus demonstrated this internal mercy. Seeing the misery of our separation from God, he showed us the greatest possible mercy by becoming one like us, taking on our sins, and dying on the cross so that we might receive forgiveness and inherit the gift of eternal life.

Jesus disapproved of the Pharisees' sacrifices, therefore, because they only complied with the law superficially. Like the Pharisees, we can offer sacrifices repeatedly and still experience no internal change of heart. When we turn away from selfish desires and seek the merciful love of God, on the other hand, we discover the internal dimension of the new covenant sealed by the blood of Christ.

This inner mercy that Jesus wants to give us comes only through his cross, as the Holy Spirit reveals to us Jesus' selfless love. The sacrifice of the cross is greater than any sacrifice offered under the old covenant (see Matthew 12:6; Hebrews 10:11-14). Through the cross we receive merciful hearts filled with compassion to serve God and neighbor.

1. What was the general attitude of the Pharisees in this passage when it came to the law? What was the essence of Jesus' reply to the Pharisees?

_____

_____

_____

2. Jesus ranked exercising mercy and doing works of mercy above other religious practices. What do you consider your highest spiritual priorities?

_____

_____

_____

3. In what ways have you made mercy a guiding principle in your life? How have others experienced the love and compassion of God through you?

_____

_____

_____

Matthew 12:9-13: Righteousness by Faith

Most of the Pharisees were strongly committed to leading righteous lives before God. But their outward acts did not necessarily reflect transformed hearts or lead to inner openness to God. Consequently, they refused to recognize that Jesus was God's agent at work to establish God's kingdom. And by holding strictly to the letter of the law, they failed to recognize that mercy superseded the law's restrictions. Jesus often admonished them for this very thing, calling them "blind guides" and "hypocrites" (Matthew 23:24, 25) who loved to justify themselves in the sight of others (see Luke 16:15). Their acts of piety served only to glorify themselves, not God.

We must move beyond the righteousness of the Pharisees (see Matthew 5:20). But Paul wrote, "There is no one who is righteous, not even one" (Romans 3:10). He meant that the only possible righteousness for us comes from God through his grace, as a free and generous gift. This righteousness Jesus gained for us through the cross; it does not come from ourselves but, rather, through our faith and baptism into Christ. Only when we have put our own wills to death, only when we have stopped dictating to ourselves how we will accomplish our own salvation, and only when we give up our own quest for righteousness will we truly discover the righteousness of Christ—and the freedom to love with the mercy and compassion of Christ. Renouncing all self-righteousness, we rejoice with Paul, "I have been crucified with Christ; and it is no longer I who live, but it is Christ who lives in me" (Galatians 2:19-20).

1. Jesus healed on the Sabbath, the day of rest. What does this suggest to you about his love for humanity? About his reverence for the Sabbath?

_____

_____

_____

2. Examine your religious practices and devotions. How do they help you—or possibly hinder you—from loving God and others? Do you need to make any adjustments?

_____

_____

_____

3. How do you honor and observe Sunday as the Lord's day? Do you know of people who will not have adequate food, shelter, or clothing this coming Sunday? Consider serving them.

_____

_____

_____

Matthew 12:14-21: Recognizing the Messiah

Knowing that the Pharisees were plotting to kill him, Jesus withdrew from their presence rather than confront them; his hour had not yet come. Some have speculated that Jesus did not want his healings to be publicized because he knew the people might rally around him at the wrong time and for the wrong reasons.

Similarly, Jesus withheld from openly proclaiming himself to be the long-awaited Messiah. Most Jews expected a triumphant political messiah through whom God would intervene to fulfill the hope of a Jewish empire. Surely Jesus didn't want to convey the impression that he was such a messiah. In 12:18-21, Matthew cited one of the servant passages from Isaiah (see 42:1-4) to suggest the type of messiah that Jesus really was. This Messiah would have the Spirit of God rest upon him. He would proclaim justice to the Gentiles. He would not make a name for himself for power or wealth. He would harm no one, not even the weakest (bruised reed). And the Gentiles would find hope in his name.

The messianic future, in the eyes of most Jews, revolved around the restoration of the kingdom of Israel, even though there was little agreement on how this would be accomplished. In later Judaism, there arose the expectation of two messiahs—a Davidic, royal messiah, and a priestly messiah of the order of Aaron or Levi. Consider how Jesus, the son of David (see Matthew 1:1) and eternal high priest (see Hebrews 7:21–8:6), perfectly fulfilled both expectations when he established his kingdom—the Israel of God.

1. Jesus came to inaugurate the kingdom of God, and yet he wanted those whom he healed to be quiet about it (see Matthew 12:15-16). What does this seem to imply?

_____

_____

_____

2. Read the servant passages from Isaiah (42:1-7; 49:1-6; 50:4-9; and 52:13–53:12). How do these passages help you understand Jesus' actions here in chapter 12 and throughout Matthew?

_____

_____

_____

3. What signs of the kingdom of God do you see around you? How might you imitate Jesus by proclaiming justice without crying aloud or without breaking "a bruised reed" (Matthew 12:20)?

_____

_____

_____

Matthew 12:22-37: Destroying Satan's Reign

Matthew's gospel gradually reveals more and more of Jesus' true identity. In this passage, Jesus faced a serious charge from scribes who asserted that he is possessed by "Beelzebul" (a demonic title meaning "lord of the flies"). They accused him of exorcising demons by "the ruler of the demons" (Matthew 12:24). Jesus exposed the fallacy of their indictment by asking, "If Satan casts out Satan, he is divided against himself; how then will his kingdom stand?" (12:26). Out of jealousy and self-righteousness, the scribes had become blind to the obvious: by casting out demons and healing people, Jesus was *destroying* Satan's kingdom, not *building* it.

To his detractors who made such charges, Jesus solemnly warned, "Whoever speaks against the Holy Spirit will not be forgiven" (Matthew 12:32). In essence, he warned them not to twist the truth by refusing God's gift of salvation and by placing others at risk, as well. Jesus had come to establish the kingdom of God by first plundering the house of the "strong man" (Matthew 12:29).

Matthew combined this rejection story with a series of skeptical responses. The sequence has a cumulative effect. Jesus' identity emerges more clearly because he refuted the negative caricatures painted by his opponents. At the same time, Matthew provided a striking contradiction: the scribes and religious authorities—whom we would expect to have welcomed Jesus—rejected him. The disciples and the crowds of simple, poor people—perhaps because of their neediness, but certainly because of their openness—saw Jesus as the Messiah, inaugurating the reign of God in power.

1. Jesus left no room for misinterpreting his identity—he is of God, not Beelzebul. Why do you think the Pharisees and scribes refused to recognize Jesus' true identity? What warnings did Jesus give them in Matthew 12:30-32 and 33-34?

_____

_____

_____

2. What interventions into your life do you recognize as signs that God's kingdom is breaking in? What indications do you see around you that the works of evil are being overturned?

_____

_____

_____

3. Jesus said that "the tree is known by its fruit" (Matthew 12:33). What good fruit are you bearing? Is there anything you need to change in your life to avoid bearing bad fruit? If so, how can you make this change?

_____

_____

_____

Matthew 12:38-42: The Sign of the Cross

The Jews in New Testament times expected the messianic age to be ushered in with spectacular signs and miracles. They awaited a messiah who would lead the nation in triumph over the Gentiles. During his ministry in Galilee (see Matthew 8–10), Jesus performed many signs and wonders, such as healing a leper and bringing a girl who had died back to life. Despite these signs and wonders, the scribes and Pharisees came to Jesus demanding still more signs, in an attempt to test his authenticity as the expected messiah (see 12:38).

Jesus rebuked them for their unbelief. He countered that if the Ninevites (a people hated for their savagery and ungodliness—see Nahum 1:1–3:19) had repented at the preaching of Jonah, and if the Queen of Sheba had traveled great distances to hear the wisdom of Solomon, should not God's people respond to an even greater one in their midst? In response to their doubt, Jesus offered only the "sign of Jonah." By this he meant that he would spend three days in the bowels of the earth before rising to life in victory over death. The crucified Jesus rising out of the tomb, bearing witness to the Father's love, would be the ultimate sign.

In every generation, God calls his people to himself and transforms them by the work of the cross. As Paul wrote, "We have been buried with him by baptism into death, so that, just as Christ was raised from the dead by the glory of the Father, so we too might walk in newness of life" (Romans 6:4). The cross of Christ, whose power transforms lives, is the sign Christ gives us today.

1. What characterizes the difference between faith based on trust and belief in God and knowledge based on signs or scientific evidence? What does the scribes' and Pharisees' demand for a sign (see Matthew 12:38) indicate about their spiritual posture?

_____

_____

_____

2. In what ways does Jesus' fulfillment of the sign of Jonah call you to greater faith in him? To deeper repentance? In what ways does it inspire you to a resurrection hope and a life of Christian service?

_____

_____

_____

3. Jesus said that "something greater than Solomon is here" (Matthew 12:42). Explain in your own words some characteristics of Jesus' "greatness." What aspect of his greatness has had the most impact on you personally? Why?

_____

_____

_____

When the unclean spirit returned to the "house" where he had formerly taken up residence, he found it "empty, swept, and put in order" (Matthew 12:44). Unfortunately, the previously possessed man had not replaced evil with good; no fundamental change had taken residence in him, which made it possible for seven additional spirits, far more evil than the original one, to dwell in him.

Jesus said, "So will it be also with this evil generation" (Matthew 12:45). Presumably, Jesus was referring to those who opposed him during his time on earth, including some of the leading Pharisees. They had witnessed Jesus' miracles continually—the expelling of demons, many healings, the multiplication of food. Yet they went on living as they had before, without a life-changing conversion to discipleship in Christ. Their hearts were empty of love, and this emptiness—like a vacuum—allowed sin to rush in.

If we want to be Jesus' disciples, we cannot simply chase evil out of our lives. We must replace sin with goodness; the very life of Christ must take up residence in our whole being. "Put on the whole armor of God, so that you may be able to stand against the wiles of the devil," Paul advises in Ephesians 6:11. This armor included the breastplate of righteousness, the shield of faith, the helmet of salvation, and the sword of the Spirit, "which is the word of God" (6:17). Thus equipped, we can persevere with God's grace to obtain the victory.

1. How is the story of the return of the unclean spirit a metaphor for morality without God?

_____

_____

_____

2. How has your robust faith in God helped ward off evil in your life? What are some examples from your experience? What other spiritual "weapons" and "armor" do you use against evil?

_____

_____

_____

3. After repenting and receiving forgiveness for sin, how can you ensure that you keep your life closed to a return to old ways and fill it with grace and goodness? What virtue would you especially like to grow in? How could you foster this growth?

_____

_____

_____

Matthew 12:46-50: God's Spiritual Family

Do we know who we are? Anthropologists tell us we are mammals who can trace our ancestry through the apes. Economists tell us we are consumers with particular buying habits. Demographers tell us we are population statistics. Scripture, however, tells us we are people of God.

"Who is my mother, and who are my brothers?" (Matthew 12:48). At first glance, in this incident, it may seem that Jesus was rebuking his blood relations. In fact, he paid the highest compliment to his mother, Mary. It is Mary, more than anyone else, who provided us with the perfect example of obedience to the Father's will: "Here am I, the servant of the Lord; let it be with me according to your word" (Luke 1:38). Mary's heartfelt response to God demonstrated her assent to following his will, which is the meaning of discipleship in Christ and, therefore, membership in God's family.

Jesus does not disown his blood relations; rather, he blesses all those who have answered God's call to membership in a new family—the church. Through this blessing, God views us as his children—brothers and sisters to his Son. Through obedience to God and his word, we affirm our membership in his family, which was initiated at baptism.

Jesus authorizes his followers to claim a new identification—as brothers and sisters in Christ. What a wonderful privilege! God considers us, mere mortals, as members in the lineage of his Son, Jesus.

1. What does this passage add to your understanding of the importance of faith and obedience to God? Of what it means to be family, community, and body of Christ?

   _____

   _____

   _____

2. What implications does Jesus' definition of his "brothers and sisters" (Matthew 12:50) have for you? How would a broader understanding of "family" help you to become a more loving person not only to your immediate family but also to your neighbors, fellow parishioners, immigrants, and strangers?

   _____

   _____

   _____

3. How do you share your faith with the members of your natural family? Who can you invite into the family of God today?

   _____

   _____

   _____

Matthew 13:1-9: Rooted in Good Soil

Jesus described four possible responses to the word of God. The seed on the footpath refers to people who quickly lose the word because they do not understand it and are led astray. The seed on rocky ground describes those with no firm roots or foundation. The seed fallen among thorns relates to those who receive the good news but later abandon it for the lure or distractions of the world. Finally, the seed on good soil describes those who hear the word of God, accept it, and live it.

Most of us like to identify ourselves with the seed planted in good soil. If we examine our lives closely, however, we may see ourselves in other parts of the story as well. Every day God asks us to decide whether or not we will live for his glory. The man who had been born blind is a great example of someone who heard the word of God, accepted it, and decided to live it. After he was healed, he joyfully glorified God—despite pressure and threats from the Pharisees (see John 9:1-38).

We all face a similar choice. We can give glory to God for his work in us, or we can allow fear and outside pressure to overcome us. We can fearlessly proclaim the marvels of God, or we can be bound by our own fears of rejection to the point that we deny God the glory due to him. Today, will we allow the gospel to transform us, or will we still try to change our own lives?

God invites us into a vibrant Christianity that transforms us and the world. If we acknowledge the action of God in our lives and desire to serve him, the seeds of faith within us will produce good fruit. We will yield thirty, sixty, or even a hundredfold for the glory of God.

1. According to this parable, what beliefs and practices does healthy and lifelong spiritual growth require?

_____

_____

_____

2. Do you recognize any ways in which God's word is choked or crowded out of your life? What could you do to ensure that your "soil" is good and that God's word takes root in you?

_____

_____

_____

3. What fruit do you see your life bearing for Christ? How might you increase your harvest?

_____

_____

_____

Matthew 13:10-17: Accepting the Message with Open Hearts

"To you it has been given to know the secrets of the kingdom of heaven, but to them it has not been given" (Matthew 13:11). Did Jesus intentionally exclude some of his listeners from understanding and accepting his message? He did use parables, stories that employ everyday situations to make a point, to get his listeners to reflect on his message and to either accept it or reject it. In fact, many of his listeners responded with hostility. Their hearts had grown dull; they had closed themselves off to the spiritual conversion Jesus had invited them to accept.

To those whose hearts are open to receive, God's word brings truth and life. An "open" heart means actively choosing to take hold of Jesus' words and apply them in our lives. Are we open to God's word and unencumbered by competing thoughts, desires, fears, and judgments? Are we actively seeking to "see" and "hear" God's truth? Jesus promised us, "Ask, and it will be given you; search, and you will find; knock, and the door will be opened for you" (Matthew 7:7).

Our understanding of this passage rests on the truth of who God is. Our God, complete and perfect in all his ways, created us for the purpose of sharing eternal life with him. His love and his desire forever remain the same for all; he wants all people to come to know him. The spiritual differences between individuals are due not to God but to our responses to God. When we see others without God in their lives, we wrongly conclude that God has withheld his truth from them. It is not a question of God's refusal to give, but of our refusal to accept. Jesus invites us to hear and see with a wholehearted understanding and a spiritual perception of the truth.

1. What did Jesus mean when he said, "Hearing they do not listen, nor do they understand" (Matthew 13:13)? If they hear, how do they not listen or understand (see 13:15)?

   _____
   _____
   _____

2. What worries, anxieties, and desires fill your ears and hinder you from listening to God's word or understanding it?

   _____
   _____
   _____

3. How can you open up more to hear the word of God? What practical steps can you take?

   _____
   _____
   _____

Matthew 13:18-23: Yielding Plentiful Fruit

Jesus often used settings and images familiar to his listeners in an effort to apply his teachings directly to their lives. The parable of the sower and the seed (see Matthew 13:3-9, 18-23) depicts everyday farm life in first-century Palestine. When Jesus explained the parable to the disciples, he said that the soil represented the varying degrees of openness we all have to the gospel message.

In the parable, the first group hears the word but doesn't understand or fully accept it (see Matthew 13:19). The second group understands but cannot stand up to the challenges of persecution or suffering (see 13:20-21). The third group hears and accepts the word but gets distracted by the world (see 13:22). The final group—the believers—hears the word, understands it, and responds to it (see 13:23).

When we first come to faith in Jesus, we begin as "infants in Christ" (1 Corinthians 3:1) who—over time—may achieve maturity. This progression from infancy to maturity does not happen through self-effort but comes through the work of the Holy Spirit in us: "For it is God who is at work in you, enabling you both to will and to work for his good pleasure" (Philippians 2:13).

With our cooperation, God will bring to completion what he has started in us, for he wants a plentiful harvest. Our response determines the yield in our lives. When we open up to Christ in our lives, he cleanses us of our sins and dead works, justifying us before God (see Hebrews 9:14; Romans 5:9). He draws us together through baptism into one body, his church, where we drink of the one Spirit and are sustained in word and sacrament (see 1 Corinthians 12:13).

1. What characterizes the person who hears the word, understands it, and bears good fruit in response to it? "Good soil" is a metaphor for what?

_____

_____

_____

2. How can participation in Sunday Mass be an example of hearing the word, understanding it, and responding to it? In what other situations do you commonly hear and respond to God's word?

_____

_____

_____

3. What else can *you* do in an effort to allow the Holy Spirit to guide you? What is *your* role?

_____

_____

_____

Matthew 13:24-30: Awaiting the Harvest

The kingdom of heaven inaugurated by Jesus "may be compared to someone who sowed good seed in his field" (Matthew 13:24). And yet, while the soil is good and the seeds are good, the enemy secretly works the field—sowing weeds (see 13:28). The weeds referred to by Jesus in this parable are a type of darnel. They commonly grow in wheat fields, but since their roots are deeper and stronger than the wheat's, any attempt to uproot them will inevitably uproot the wheat as well. Thus, if the weeds are eliminated prematurely, there will be no harvest at all.

In faith, we trust in God's perfect timing. We may long for the day when God completely destroys evil, but we know that God in his wisdom knows the best time for the harvest. In the meantime, we must endure the evil in the world.

As the Father allowed Satan to tempt Jesus (see Matthew 4:1-11), the Father also allows Satan to tempt us.

We must resist evil wherever we see it and stand up for righteousness. In this, we can depend on God's help, relying on the truth of his word, the power of his love, and his grace and strength. As the Father sent angels to minister to Jesus in the desert after his confrontation with the devil (see Matthew 4:11), we, too, can count on our Father to care for us.

Someday the weeds and the wheat will be separated. The weeds will be burned, while the wheat will be gathered together (see Matthew 13:30). At this final judgment, evil will be defeated, and "the righteous will shine like the sun in the kingdom of their Father" (13:43).

1. What does this parable reveal about Satan's nature and how he works to sow evil?

_____

_____

_____

2. What instances in today's society can you think of when it is difficult to sort out truth and error? What does the householder's response teach you about how to respond to evil? In face of the presence of evil in the world, how can you maintain hope for the coming of God's kingdom?

_____

_____

_____

3. What parable of your own would you tell someone to describe what the kingdom of heaven is like in your life?

_____

_____

_____

Matthew 13:31-35: Growth Comes from God

Jesus chose his parables carefully. He wanted the jostling masses to understand an essential point about the kingdom of God: the Father established it for *everyone*, not just the Pharisees or the Sanhedrin, the wealthy or the politically powerful. Although God's kingdom on earth, which Jesus became flesh to inaugurate, was initiated in an obscure corner of the world, among a small, inconspicuous people, he intended it for every single person ever born, all of us. It is the mystery and the wonder of God's work that what seems so insignificant has great results!

In our sometimes mundane lives, as we perform our routine tasks, we should keep this central message in the forefront of our minds: we are loved by God! Most of us tend to think of ourselves as somewhat ordinary and of what we do as relatively insignificant in the grand scheme of things. But by equating significance with recognition, we fall into the trap of thinking that our "ordinary" contribution matters relatively little. We must never underestimate what the Lord can do through us, for great things happen when "ordinary" believers respond obediently to God.

God views each and every one of us as precious. Just look at how he ushered in his kingdom on earth through a poor carpenter from a subjugated people. We each have an essential role to play in the body of Christ. Many saints, in fact, came from simple families that trusted in the Lord. Let us persevere and allow the mustard seed and leaven in our lives to grow and transform us.

1. If you could write a one-sentence thesis or theme statement about the parable of the mustard seed, what would it be?

   _____

   _____

   _____

2. What do the mustard seed and leaven communicate about the nature of the kingdom of God? Why do you think Jesus chose these images to make his point?

   _____

   _____

   _____

3. When have you seen something seemingly insignificant in the eyes of the world develop into something very significant in God's sight? In what area of your own life are you aware of God's grace transforming you?

   _____

   _____

   _____

Matthew 13:36-43: Leaving Judgment to Christ

Have you ever tried to weed a garden in which the plants were still seedlings? Unless you are a master gardener or a farmer, you probably uprooted your plants along with the weeds, and you probably could not tell the one from the other. Desirable plants and weeds can look alike, especially in their early stages; thus, weeding can result in the loss of many good plants.

Most commentators believe that this parable reflects the experience of the primitive church as it grappled with the problem of good and evil in its midst. The first believers discovered quickly that the church contained both wheat and weeds—those who lived what they professed, and those who claimed allegiance to Christ but showed no evidence of it. The desire to root out all those who showed no signs of new life had to be curbed in light of this parable.

The inclusion of this parable and Jesus' explanation in the gospel show that the church did not see itself as the final judge. God alone dispenses justice. The leaders of the early church saw that the time of harvest, the final judgment, had been delayed so that as many as possible could receive the mercy and salvation of Jesus and come into his kingdom (see 2 Peter 3:9).

Until the end of days, the church must encourage, preach, strengthen, and teach all who will listen in the hope that they might believe and be converted. Being ourselves fallen men and women, we must put aside our desire to take judgment into our own hands. Instead, we must continue to hope for Christ's life to take root in even the most dormant and hardened among us.

1. How does Jesus' explanation of the parable of the weeds add to your understanding of God's judgment and justice? To your understanding of God's love and mercy?

_____

_____

_____

2. What is your attitude toward "weeds" in the church? In the world at large? If necessary, ask the Holy Spirit to help you let go of your own need to judge others so that you can reach out to them with God's love.

_____

_____

_____

3. We try to keep our gardens and lawns well maintained and weed free. What maintenance can you do on yourself to help keep sin and evil from your life?

_____

_____

_____

Matthew 13:44-46: The Kingdom Treasure

What does being a citizen of the kingdom of heaven mean to us? Let us take a moment to think about this question before reading on.

If we do not have a deep appreciation of what citizenship in the kingdom of God means, then we will not likely consider it worth sacrificing everything in order to attain it. If, on the other hand, we know in our hearts the deep love of Jesus and how he came to rescue us from the power of sin and condemnation, we will let nothing come between ourselves and Jesus. He has forgiven our every sin as we have turned to him in repentance; he restores us to true life with the Father. If we recall these things with gratitude, we will know the treasures of the kingdom of God.

Scripture itself provides us with many examples of people who knew the worth of the kingdom and of those who did not. Consider the case of the rich young man (see Matthew 19:16-22). Jesus tested his heart by asking him to abandon his beloved worldly possessions. This question left him bereft of an answer. His wealth was more meaningful to him than Jesus; his material goods were more real to him than the promise of eternal life.

St. Paul thought in exactly the opposite direction (see Philippians 3:7-9). He considered everything a loss compared to the inestimable treasure of knowing and serving Jesus. All else was rubbish—in Greek, *skubalon*, which is literally "dung" (3:8). If we are to be like Paul and treasure the kingdom of God, we must nurture God's love in our hearts.

1. How is Jesus' description of the kingdom of heaven unlike the adage "Don't put all your eggs in one basket"? What additional light do Jesus' words in Matthew 6:21—"Where your treasure is, there your heart will be also"—shed on your understanding of this passage?

_____

_____

_____

2. Do Jesus' parables about the hidden treasure and the pearl of great price cause you to rejoice or to feel uncomfortable? Why?

_____

_____

_____

3. What have you given up to gain the treasure of God's kingdom? What more could you do to throw yourself into wholehearted devotion to God? What's holding you back?

_____

_____

_____

Matthew 13:47-52: Treasures, Old and New

Jesus maintained that "every scribe who has been trained for the kingdom of heaven" (Matthew 13:52) was a person of unique privilege. Such a person, taught according to the old covenant, would come face to face with the blessings and power of God in the gospel. Through the Holy Spirit, God could build upon such a person's knowledge of the Hebrew Scriptures to enrich him in the gospel of Christ for his own benefit and for the benefit of all the church.

The old covenant contains many elements that retain their importance under the new, and the new covenant itself needs to be understood and interpreted in light of the old. The scribe, therefore, needed to recognize and deal with his prejudices about the meaning of the whole word of God. But how did the scribe know what to cherish and use and what to throw away?

In answer to this question, Paul wrote, "But the aim of such instruction is love that comes from a pure heart, a good conscience, and sincere faith" (1 Timothy 1:5). Paul knew that what came from God would bear loving fruit among God's people. The Holy Spirit, poured out at Pentecost, would enlighten the minds and "guide [us] into all the truth" (John 16:13).

The scribe's challenge remains with us today. Since Vatican II, the church and global culture have undergone tremendous change. We continue to ask the Holy Spirit, who has bestowed on us gifts of wisdom and discernment, to help us determine what will lead us to holiness, love of God, and the building up of the church.

1. What "treasures" does the church cherish and celebrate from the old covenant?

_____

_____

_____

2. How familiar are you with Christianity's Jewish roots? What could you do to learn more about the treasures found in Judaism?

_____

_____

_____

3. What are some treasures—old and new—that you particularly value in your Christian life? What parts of your Christian heritage are especially meaningful to you? Why? What one teaching from the new covenant will you seek to apply more faithfully to your life this week?

_____

_____

_____

Matthew 13:53-58: Seeing All Things Anew

Routines help us structure our daily lives. At home, routine chores help us care for our families, eat nutritious meals, and keep our homes clean. At work or school, routine tasks and assignments help us efficiently accomplish our professional and educational goals. Routines also help us develop our relationships with God and our Christian brothers and sisters.

On the other hand, routines can become commonplace and then dull, maybe even burdensome. If we cling too hard to our routines, we may close ourselves off to new possibilities. Perhaps the townspeople of Nazareth, who had known Jesus for many years, had closed themselves off to an understanding of him beyond their routine, mundane impressions.

But Jesus broke with routine when he demonstrated wisdom and miraculous powers among them (see Matthew 13:54). Even so, "they took offense at him" and found him altogether too much for them (13:57). They were unable to recognize the Son of God in their midst, because they clung to their own preconceived notions of the Jesus they had known as a boy and young adult. So Jesus "did not do many deeds of power there, because of their unbelief" (13:58).

Sometimes we develop similar attitudes that limit the work of God among us. We get accustomed to a Christianity in which God does not speak, healings do not occur, and nothing ever changes—so we think. We too easily forget the words of Scripture and the testimony of countless saints that gives witness to Christ alive in them. Expectant faith calls us to see anew the work of God in our midst.

1. What have you learned from this passage about God's presence in the midst of our routine lives? How does this passage affect your outlook on the "ordinariness" of your own life?

_____

_____

_____

2. What do you imagine Jesus felt when many from his hometown rejected him? Why does rejection hurt more when it comes from people we know and love?

_____

_____

_____

3. What could you do to move beyond "routine" belief in Jesus and stir up more expectant faith to see him work powerfully in your life?

_____

_____

_____

Matthew 14:1-12: The Courage to Follow Christ

John the Baptist both terrified and fascinated Herod. Although Herod had thrown John in prison, he sensed that the people were right: John was a prophet (see Matthew 14:5). And so Herod "was grieved" (14:9) when he found that to fulfill his reckless oath he had to have John beheaded.

Although John the Baptist endured a tragic death, he had done his work on earth—he had gone "before the Lord to prepare his ways" (Luke 1:76). Jesus described him as greater than any born of women (see Matthew 11:11). Herod, on the other hand, was far more pitiable than John. He had been given the honor of knowing one of the greatest prophets of all time, yet instead of being transformed, he chose to continue in his sinful ways. Instead of grasping the truth, Herod would forever be known as the man who killed John the Baptist.

Fear of change often leads us to hold on to negative and sinful patterns in our lives. Because we have the honor of knowing Jesus Christ on a personal basis, we have the opportunity to put fear aside and to rejoice. The Lord calls us to a committed Christianity that can change our lives in awesome ways. Will we give up our sinful habits and worldly fears that lead us away from God? Will we risk persecution by taking the unpopular stands Christ calls us to take?

"We are not among those who shrink back and so are lost, but among those who have faith and so are saved" (Hebrews 10:39). Let us not draw back from the Lord; his truth is the door to eternal life.

1. Note the various emotions attributed to Herod in this passage. In what ways did Herod allow himself to be ruled by his emotions? What were the consequences for each person involved in this scene?

   _____

   _____

   _____

2. How might Herod have acted differently if he hadn't let his own vanity and false sense of "rightness" get in the way of doing the truly right thing (see Matthew 14:9)? When has the strength of your conscience helped you to make a difficult decision or behave in a Christian manner?

   _____

   _____

   _____

3. John the Baptist was a person unafraid to direct all his energies toward serving Christ and proclaiming truth. What fears hinder you from following Christ? What could help you overcome these fears?

   _____

   _____

   _____

Matthew 14:13-21: The Abundance of Grace

Not all at once, but little by little, the Lord calls us, even in times when we do not expect or even notice his call. He may begin with a whispered question in our hearts or with one of life's little annoyances. As the whispers and annoyances persist, they pile up until they force us to ask ourselves who we are and who our God is. We soon become aware of an eternal perspective, of the big picture, and even then we may not realize God has been moving within us.

Little by little, we begin to respond in ways that we never would have before. Maybe we start going to Mass during the week, or we start reading Scripture on a daily basis. Very often we begin a deeper and more direct walk with Jesus in these seemingly small ways—all in response to God's persistent love and mercy for us.

God's love never ceases working in our lives. Jesus demonstrated this constant work on our behalf when he miraculously fed the five thousand. The disciples suggested dismissing the crowd, but Jesus hadn't finished caring for them. His generosity and graciousness far surpass anything we can imagine, and he freely gives to anyone who comes to him.

Let us turn to God and allow his abundant grace to heal us and make us sons and daughters who reflect his love in all we do and say. When we next humbly receive the bread of life, let us ask Jesus for everything he wants to give us. God's provision for us is boundless and immeasurable. Let nothing stand in his way today—no grudges, no anger, no bitterness, and no sinful habits.

1. What does the abundant quantity of the leftovers after Jesus multiplied the loaves and fish reveal about God's nature?

_____

_____

_____

2. In what ways does the miracle of feeding the five thousand, especially verse 19, point to the Eucharist?

_____

_____

_____

3. When has God asked you to use what seemed to you like your meager resources to meet the needs of others? What happened when you responded to God?

_____

_____

_____

Matthew 14:22-36: Trusting in the Lord

The Sea of Galilee is actually a lake (approximately thirteen by eight miles), and it is almost completely surrounded by mountains. When the northern winds funnel down through these mountains, they sweep violently across the lake, causing fierce waves. In the midst of such a storm, Jesus manifested his power to the disciples by walking on the water.

Just prior to this event, Jesus had multiplied the loaves and fish. One would think that the disciples, having just seen this demonstration of Jesus' power, would have confidence in his ability to save them from the fury of the storm. Instead, they were terrified (see Matthew 14:26), and only Peter, having seen the power of Jesus' words and actions, put his faith in him and began to walk on the water (see 14:29).

In this incident, Peter experienced the trial and growth of a true disciple of Christ. By stepping out of the boat at the Lord's invitation, Peter demonstrated his growing realization that Jesus was the Messiah. Even when his faith faltered and he began to sink, Peter still cried out to Jesus, saying, "Lord, save me" (Matthew 14:30). After these extraordinary events, all the disciples worshipped Jesus in awe, saying, "Truly you are the Son of God" (14:33).

Day after day, the Son of God confronts us with situations that test our faith in him. Especially during life's storms, our faith may falter. We may at first doubt that God cares for us, or even that he exists, but these very trials beckon us all the more to place our faith in Jesus, to call out to him for strength, to grow in our faith that Christ saves us from drowning in doubt.

1. Why do you think the disciples failed to recognize Jesus as he walked across the water?

_____

_____

_____

2. Recall a time when Jesus called you to "step out on the water" in faith. How did Jesus hold you up as you took this step?

_____

_____

_____

3. What "storms" in your life have caused you to doubt Jesus' love and care for you? How did Jesus "rescue" you from sinking when you called out to him? What could help you persevere in faith?

_____

_____

_____

Matthew 15:1-20: Wholehearted Devotion to God

How radiant people look when they're in love! Just by looking at their faces, we can see the joy in their hearts. In a similar way, our actions reveal our attitudes. Often we can see how people feel about themselves or about certain political or social issues just by observing their everyday actions. But this is especially true concerning our attitudes toward God. If we have Christ in us, his love and peace shine through, even if we are quiet about our inner lives.

The Pharisees were expert at instituting and adhering to regulations based on ancient traditions. Yet for some of them, their hearts were far from the God of their ancestors. As these Pharisees did, we may confuse ritual piety with true godliness and confuse observance of traditions with inner purity. When observance becomes an end in itself, we miss out on the promised joy and peace of Christ.

God made us unified persons with bodies designed to express what is in our hearts, and with hearts intimately tied up with our relationships in the world. God takes a deep interest in the way we express our hearts with one another. When we express ourselves with harsh words or an angry tongue (see Matthew 15:11), we need to understand that our hearts need purification by the Lord.

Jesus said that the greatest commandment is to wholeheartedly love God and, subsequently, to love our neighbors as ourselves (see Mark 12:28-31). With such love as our primary concern, we walk the path toward purity of heart, derive life and nourishment from our observances, and relate to others with sincerity and love.

1. In your own words, what does Jesus' teaching mean to you: "What comes out of the mouth proceeds from the heart" (Matthew 15:18)?

_____

_____

_____

2. What does your speech reveal about your heart? Do you gossip? Do you lie? Do you offer kind words? What can you do to stop yourself from talking negatively about other people or from speaking harsh or rude words at all?

_____

_____

_____

3. How do your devotional practices strengthen your relationship with God? Is there any way that they are blocking your relationship with God or that they are a substitute for obeying him?

_____

_____

_____

The story of how Jesus rewarded the Canaanite woman's faith—a testimony to God's love for all people in all nations—has brought hope and comfort to hurting souls in every age of the church. Today, when we wonder if there is any hope for us sinners, we can find confident assurance in the Canaanite woman's faith. Isaiah writes, "My house shall be called a house of prayer for *all* peoples" (56:7, emphasis added)—no one is excluded.

When this woman heard that Jesus had come to her town, her heart must have leapt in anticipation. She had probably heard stories about his miraculous works. As she approached him—presumably with a mixture of desperation and hope—she cried out, "Have mercy on me, Lord, Son of David; my daughter is tormented by a demon" (Matthew 15:22). Before making her request, she paid him homage, showing herself to be one of the foreigners who "join themselves to the LORD . . . to love the name of the LORD, and to be his servants" (Isaiah 56:6).

When Jesus told her that he had been sent "only to the lost sheep of the house of Israel" (Matthew 15:24), she pressed on in faith, saying, "Lord, help me. . . . even the dogs eat the crumbs that fall from their masters' table" (15:25, 27). Moved by her humility and her conviction that he could heal her daughter, Jesus rewarded her faith (see 15:28). Thus it was that an "outsider"—a Gentile—received the blessings of Yahweh, the God of Israel.

God does not limit his power and desire to bless only the few. We can enter into the healing presence of Jesus as we praise and worship God, imitating the Canaanite woman's adoration.

1. What adjectives best describe the Canaanite woman's faith? What other virtues did she exhibit in addition to faith?

_____

_____

_____

2. What qualities of the Canaanite woman would you most like to imitate in your own life? Why? How could you foster these qualities?

_____

_____

_____

3. What lesson does this incident teach you about approaching the Father in prayer? Recall a time when God seemed to give you a "no" in answer to a prayer request. How did you continue your prayer-dialogue with God then?

_____

_____

_____

Matthew 15:29-39: Miracles—Past, Present, and Future

The miracles that Jesus performed in his life on earth bore witness both to him and to his Father. His signs and wonders revealed the arrival of the promised Messiah. As a result, the people "praised the God of Israel" (Matthew 15:31). These great events, like the healing of the sick and the feeding of the four thousand, are an invitation to all of us to believe.

During our lifetime, we may have witnessed miracles ourselves, perhaps the healing of a very ill person who had not been expected to recover. We also know of cases in which a healing did not occur, even though many people had been praying for one. Regarding these cases, we do well to remember that the miracles Jesus performed during his time on earth and the miracles that continue to occur in our own day are only a foreshadowing of far greater things to come.

The *Catechism of the Catholic Church* points out that the signs and wonders accompanying Jesus' words reveal the kingdom of God made present in him. "By freeing some individuals from the earthly evils of hunger, injustice, illness and death, Jesus performed messianic signs" (549). These signs invite us not only to believe in Jesus the Messiah but also to step with our whole mind, heart, and strength into the kingdom of God, which Jesus made available to us all when he rose from the dead and freed us from sin and death forever.

The ultimate miracle was Christ's resurrection and all that it does for us. When we pass from this earth and meet the Lord, we, too, will experience that same miracle of resurrection.

1. What typified the crowds' responses to Jesus in Matthew 15:30-31? How is your own response to Jesus similar? Different?

_____

_____

_____

2. What aspect of Jesus' feeding of the four thousand speaks most strongly to you at this point in your life? Jesus' compassion? His generosity? The eucharistic imagery? Why?

_____

_____

_____

3. What would be the ultimate miracle for Christ to perform in your own life?

_____

_____

_____

Matthew 16:1-12: Asking for Signs

Because we have faith in Jesus as God's Son, we may tend to overlook the fact that as a man he experienced the same human emotions we experience. How surprising his expressed disappointment when "he sighed deeply in his spirit" (Mark 8:12)! But Jesus knew the Pharisees thoughts (see Luke 9:47); they meant "to test Jesus" with a demand for a sign (Matthew 16:1). Here, all the synoptic gospel writers reveal Jesus as one like us, frustrated by the skepticism of others.

In the Old Testament, God strengthened the faith of his people by reminding them of past signs (such as the Exodus), by providing them with present signs, and by encouraging them with prophecies of future signs. Many of them expected the messianic days to provide signs and wonders at least equal to those in the Exodus, in particular, victory over the pagans.

Unlike the Israelites in the desert, Jesus refused to tempt God by asking for signs on his own account, or to satisfy those who asked for signs in order to test him. Jesus may have disappointed the expectations of the Pharisees and Sadducees, but he fulfilled them perfectly from a spiritual perspective: he announced the dawning of true salvation through the great sign of his being lifted up in glory on the cross.

What expectations for signs do we lay at Jesus' feet today? Do we acknowledge his saving death and resurrection as the supreme sign in our lives? Or do we seek to put him to the test by demanding signs that suit us? Have we placed our deepest trust in him and truly believed his words that the "Father knows what you need before you ask him" (Matthew 6:8)?

1. Why do you think the Pharisees and Sadducees wanted to test Jesus? Why did Jesus refuse their demand for a sign?

_____

_____

_____

2. Have you ever asked Jesus for a sign? If so, why? What was his response? What does Jesus' answer to the Pharisees and Sadducees mean to you personally?

_____

_____

_____

3. In what "signs of the times" (Matthew 16:3) do you recognize God's action in the world today?

_____

_____

_____

Matthew 16:13-20: The Christ, the Son of the Living God

Much of Matthew's gospel deals with the question of faith, and it offers a climactic answer with the proclamation of Jesus as "the Messiah, the Son of the living God" (Matthew 16:16). In Matthew's account, Peter described Jesus as "the Son of the living God," a phrase not found in Mark's report of this incident (see Mark 8:29). Some Scripture scholars, comparing these two versions, conjecture that Mark may have preserved Peter's original words, while Matthew, drawing on a slightly later and more developed understanding of Jesus from the early church, provided the fuller description. The important point for us to glean from this is that faith does not remain static, nor does it stagnate; faith grows and develops in depth and understanding.

The dawning of faith brings us to the spiritual insight that causes us to utter a proclamation similar to Peter's. And while it is one thing to recognize Jesus as the Messiah, anointed by God to save his people, the deepening of faith brings us to the understanding of Jesus as God, possessing all the transcendent qualities of the godhead, coequal with the Father and the Holy Spirit.

Who indeed can fully know God? Not one of us in a hundred lifetimes! And what could we ever give God that would lead us to expect such a reward in return (see Romans 11:34-35)? From the overflowing riches of God, however, we come to know the identity of Jesus so that we may proclaim him Messiah, the Son of the living God. Through the indwelling Holy Spirit, we continually grow in desire to deepen in this knowledge, and we long for the fullness of revelation that will be ours when we join with him for all eternity.

1. Peter called Jesus "the Messiah, the Son of the living God" (Matthew 16:16). What does this suggest to you about the state of Peter's faith in Jesus? How did Peter reach this understanding of Jesus?

   _____

   _____

   _____

2. How would you personally answer Jesus' question, "Who do you say that I am?" (Matthew 16:15)? How does your life give concrete witness to your answer?

   _____

   _____

   _____

3. What indications do you see in your life that your faith has grown and matured over the past few years? What has given—and continues to give—this growth impetus?

   _____

   _____

   _____

Matthew 16:21-28: The Difficult Wisdom of the Cross

Jesus shocked his disciples when he told them that he must suffer and die in Jerusalem. They simply could not conceive of God abandoning his servant—the one whom Peter had just proclaimed "the Messiah, the Son of the living God" (Matthew 16:16). It made no sense! Yet when Peter objected, Jesus sharply rebuked him: "Get behind me, Satan! You are a stumbling block to me; for you are setting your mind not on divine things but on human things" (16:23).

Peter, like many of the prophets, struggled to understand God's ways. When Jeremiah responded to God's call to warn the Israelites of their imminent punishment, their religious leaders rejected and physically abused him (see Jeremiah 20:1-2). In his confusion, Jeremiah confessed his bitterness: "O LORD, you have enticed me. . . . / I have become a laughingstock all day long" (20:7).

The call to discipleship—which both Peter and Jeremiah experienced—is a privilege and a challenge. The privilege rests in the disciple's close relationship with a loving God, a wellspring of blessings. The challenge comes in denying ourselves and taking up the cross with Jesus (see Matthew 16:24), that is, traveling the road that leads to such a relationship with God. Despite their initial inability to grasp God's ways, both Jeremiah and Peter persisted in obedience. In the end, they became shining beacons, reflecting the glory of their beloved Master. By allowing God to work in our hearts, we, too, can open a pathway for God to bless us and form us as his disciples.

1. Why do you think Peter still failed to understand Jesus? In what ways are you like Peter? What lesson does Jesus' response to Peter teach you?

   _____

   _____

   _____

2. What do Jesus' statements in this passage say about the earthly and spiritual reality in which we live?

   _____

   _____

   _____

3. In concrete terms, how have you denied yourself and taken up Jesus' cross (see Matthew 16:24)? What have you gained by your persistence of faith and your obedience?

   _____

   _____

   _____

Matthew 17:1-9: Transformed into the Image of Christ

The apostles who were present at the transfiguration had the awesome privilege to see Jesus as he would appear in his glory at the right hand of the Father. The holy, transforming light that they saw Jesus clothed in overwhelmed their senses. It came not from outside Jesus, as if the sun were shining on him, but from within him, from the grace of God transforming his human body.

God wants to transform us, just as he transformed his Son; he has "saved us and called us with a holy calling" (2 Timothy 1:9). Too often, however, we want to change ourselves, following our own plan and using our own means. This doesn't work. Spiritual change begins in faith. When the Spirit sees our faith, he begins to transform us and give us a share in Christ's perfect holiness.

God desires that all members of the church of Christ reflect his glory and, by this reflection, change the world. Through his Spirit, the Father transforms us all into radiant sons and daughters. Ever since God promised Abram to make of him "a great nation" (Genesis 12:2), God has been working to bring his people to that fullness of life that will renew the face of the earth.

Jesus' transfiguration helped prepare the apostles for the salvation he was to win for all humanity. The Spirit's transformation within us and the church prepares the world to receive and accept the salvation Jesus has won for us. We must allow the Holy Spirit to work within and through us, molding us into the image of Christ. As we are transformed, the church reflects more and more of God's glory, through which the whole world is touched to the heart.

1. Why do you think Jesus allowed Peter, James, and John to see this revelation of his glory? How did this vision affect them? Why did Jesus command them not to tell others of his transfiguration (see Matthew 17:9)?

_____

_____

_____

2. In what ways does your life reflect God's glory for others to see? Is there anything that casts a shadow over its brightness? If so, ask the Holy Spirit to continue his transforming work in you.

_____

_____

_____

3. The heavenly voice told the three disciples, "This is my Son, the beloved; . . . listen to him!" (Matthew 17:5). How attentive are you when Jesus speaks to you? What could you do to improve your ability to listen to him?

_____

_____

_____

Matthew 17:10-13: Recognizing the Messiah

During this time in Israel, many Jews clung to the hope that God would carry out his plan to save his people and that his instrument would be the Messiah, the Son of David. Widespread messianic speculation, coupled with dreams of temporal glory for Israel, had their sure source in prophecies like the prophet Malachi's, which said that a forerunner would announce the time of God's intervention in human history: "See, I am sending my messenger to prepare the way before me, and the Lord whom you seek will suddenly come to his temple" (Malachi 3:1); and "Lo, I will send you the prophet Elijah before the great and terrible day of the LORD comes. He will turn the hearts of parents to their children and the hearts of children to their parents" (4:5-6).

Jesus told his disciples that this prophecy had already been fulfilled in the person of John the Baptist. When John's birth was foretold to his father, Zechariah, the angel Gabriel declared that John would go before him "with the spirit and power of Elijah . . . to turn the hearts of parents to their children" (Luke 1:17).

The Jews did not recognize John the Baptist as the new Elijah and, consequently, did not acknowledge Jesus as the promised Messiah. The word of God confronts us with the same question that perplexed the people of Jesus' time: "Who do people say that [Jesus] is?" (see Matthew 16:13). If he is merely a moral leader to emulate, then he will not be vital to our lives. But if we say that he is truly the Messiah, whose death and resurrection has saved us, then the only possible response is to commit our lives to following him.

1. Why do you think Matthew felt it important to include this passage in his gospel text?

_____

_____

_____

2. What role do you see John the Baptist fulfilling in Matthew's gospel?

_____

_____

_____

3. How does John the Baptist's role as described in Scripture (see Matthew 3:1-3; Luke 3:1-18) continue to affect you today?

_____

_____

_____

Matthew 17:14-21: Faith as a Grain of Mustard Seed

Most of us say we have faith—that is, we believe in God. A problem arises when we fail to apply what faith we have to our daily circumstances. We see this when a crisis occurs, such as poor health, the death of a loved one, or loss of a job, and we begin to grow fearful. Fear leads us to question whether God really loves us. We wonder whether the Spirit truly dwells in us, as he promised.

In times of trial, we tend to rely more on the seen than the unseen, and this signals a weak faith. Jesus' disciples also suffered from "little faith" (Matthew 17:20). They had begun to follow Jesus, but they had not placed their whole trust in him. Jesus says, "If you have faith the size of a mustard seed, you will say to this mountain, 'Move from here to there,' and it will move" (17:20).

To have such faith, and for that faith to grow robust, we must allow God to cultivate it. Since "faith is the assurance of things hoped for, the conviction of things not seen" (Hebrews 11:1), we need to do things, such as pray, which make us aware of unseen realities. Mother Teresa said, "Has your faith grown? If you do not pray, your faith will leave you" (*Total Surrender*).

Prayer helps us grow in faith by turning our attention toward Jesus, not toward ourselves—by focusing us on his promises, not on our own feelings. It helps us to have "conviction of things not seen" (Hebrews 11:1) and to ask for the grace to trust in him. Let us pray for a deeper faith.

1. What can you learn from how the father in this passage approached Jesus (see Matthew 17:14-15)?

   _____

   _____

   _____

2. When Jesus said that we could move mountains if only we had the slightest faith, he wasn't saying we can have superhuman strength. So what do you think he was saying?

   _____

   _____

   _____

3. What challenge or difficulty are you currently facing in your life? How might you approach Jesus and ask for faith the size of a mustard seed to "move" this "mountain"? Do it.

   _____

   _____

   _____

Matthew 17:22-27: The Son of Man Who Reigns

Matthew often focuses our attention on the way in which the disciples were coming to know Jesus' full identity (see Matthew 13:54–17:27). They had seen him feed the multitudes from a few loaves and fishes (see 14:13-21); they had seen him walk on water (see 14:26); they had seen him heal many with physical illnesses (see 14:34-36); and they had seen him cast out a demon (see 17:14-20).

As if this were not enough, Peter, James, and John saw Jesus transfigured on a mountaintop and heard the voice of God proclaim, "This is my Son, the Beloved" (Matthew 17:5). Through these signs and actions, the disciples came to believe that Jesus was the Messiah, the Son of God, who had come to save the people. And Jesus confirmed this reality by his words to his disciples.

The passion prediction and the story of the temple tax gave the disciples two more key insights into Jesus' identity (see Matthew 17:22-23, 24-27). First, Jesus proclaimed himself the "Son of Man," a reference to Daniel's vision of a heavenly being who would be given "dominion and glory and kingship, that all peoples, nations, and languages should serve him" (Daniel 7:14).

Second, Jesus compared himself to the children of kings, who are not obligated to pay taxes to their father (see Matthew 17:25). Therefore, Jesus didn't have to pay the religious tax for the upkeep of the temple—he was the Son of him whose temple it was! Thus, Jesus was more than just a healer or a preacher; he was more than just a miracle worker. He was, and is, the Messiah, destined to reign over all people forever; he was, and is, the Son of almighty God.

1. While Jesus revealed his identity more and more, the disciples were still "distressed" upon hearing again of Jesus' upcoming death (see Matthew 17:23). What does this seem to imply?

_____

_____

_____

2. Do you find Jesus' death for salvation distressing? Why or why not? How do you feel about the resurrection?

_____

_____

_____

3. Why do you think Jesus paid the temple tax (see Matthew 17:24-27)? What does the fact that Jesus paid the tax indicate about him and his attitude toward the law?

_____

_____

_____

Matthew 18:1-11: Developing a Spirit of Humility

"Unless you change and become like children, you will never enter the kingdom of heaven" (Matthew 18:3). Jesus did not teach us to become childish; he meant, rather, that becoming "like children" involves being humble and turning to God in trust, as one would to a loving father. In such a relationship with God, we grow in our ability to exhibit qualities such as trust, admiration, and confidence. We experience an increasing desire to please God through our openness to his guiding presence, knowing and believing that he cares about our needs, desires, and our search for fulfillment.

Most important, Jesus taught us here to turn from our proud ways and approach our heavenly Father like the prodigal son and say, "Father, I have sinned against heaven and before you; I am no longer worthy to be called your son" (Luke 15:21). As we humbly acknowledge him as our loving Father and confess our sins to him with truthfulness and sorrow, we step onto the path toward humility and salvation.

The tendency of the world is to scorn the humble, to see humility as a sign of a weak will or disposition. To the contrary, Jesus warned us, "Take care that you do not despise one of these little ones" (Matthew 18:10). He meant that God loves the humble because only the humble acknowledge his ability to care and nurture. For this reason, Jesus has promised us, "Blessed are the poor in spirit, for theirs is the kingdom of heaven" (5:3). God wants all of his disciples to turn to him like trusting children, for his desire is that none should be lost. "For the Son of Man came to save the lost" (18:11).

1. In what ways did Jesus emphasize the seriousness of his mission in this passage? What challenging call is Jesus presenting to you, personally, through this passage?

_____

_____

_____

2. Jesus warned us not to cause others to sin or lead them into temptation (see Matthew 18:6-7). If you have intentionally or even unintentionally done so, what could you do to remedy this and/or make amends?

_____

_____

_____

3. How might you present Christ in your own person to those who are "lost" today (see Matthew 18:11)?

_____

_____

_____

Matthew 18:12-14: The Shepherd Seeks Lost Sheep

Whether we realize it or not, we are all lost sheep, damaged by sin, and in need of healing. As St. Paul says, we were born into a life separated from God (see Romans 3:10-18). Our own green pastures—those things, places, or positions that look so good to us apart from God—ultimately leave us empty, lonely, and unfulfilled. Left unchecked, our inherited tendency to sin can plunge us into perilous despair.

Why is this so? As creations of God, made in his image, our desire is for him—and this desire can be satisfied by nothing other than God. He wills that we experience the green pastures he has in store for us, which are much different than the ones we might choose out of our fallen natures.

From the beginning of time, God has wanted to gather a people to himself. The image of the shepherd is a frequently used metaphor to describe God leading his people from peril to fullness of life. "The whole of human nature is a single sheep and you [Jesus] took it upon your shoulders" (St. Gregory of Nyssa, *On the Canticle of Canticles*).

In Christ Jesus, God gathers "the Israel of God" (Galatians 6:16) from all peoples and nations. He intends for there to be one flock and one shepherd (see John 10:16). To accomplish this, Jesus left his throne to come and save us, to free us, to give us a whole new life within him. We should cherish the new life he offers us, because he purchased it for us at the price of his own suffering, his own blood, his own death! All the more, then, God rejoices at the return of the stray sheep. He wishes that none be lost.

1. What does this parable reveal about God's nature? What does it reveal about Jesus' mission?

_____

_____

_____

2. How do you respond to the shepherd in this passage? If you are lost, do you wish to be found? Why or why not? Do you walk within arms' reach of the shepherd?

_____

_____

_____

3. Do you know anyone who has wandered away from Christ's sheepfold? What can you and perhaps others do to help bring this person back?

_____

_____

_____

Matthew 18:15-20: Reproving One Another in Love

God created us with love, and he wants to pour this very love into our hearts. Because we are his people, he desires to nourish us, guide us, and discipline us out of love. We are the delight of his heart, and all his works—his provisions, his compassion, and his guidance—are intended to lead us back to him.

Out of this same heart of love, Jesus calls us to help our brothers and sisters—to seek the best for them and to lead them to the Father. This may include saying and doing difficult things in order to protect and nurture others' relationships with God. As hard as this may be, the debt of love that we owe one another in Christ compels us (see Romans 13:8). We love because Christ first loved us; out of this love, we seek to build one another up in the Lord.

Parents oftentimes have to say difficult things to their children in order to help them grow. Most parents recognize the challenge of correcting out of love. They do so to guide their children toward Christian adulthood in order for them to receive their full inheritance and rights as children of God. In the same way, God loves and disciplines us—his beloved children.

God created us to live in unity with him and with each other. We can know this unity because God's only-begotten Son removed every dividing wall by his death on the cross. Through the gift of the Spirit, he has given us everything we need to live out this unity—to become vessels of his love and mercy.

1. By what standard and in what way are we to correct our brothers and sisters in Christ (see John 7:24)? Recall an instance when another person injured or wronged you in some way. How did you seek to repair this relationship and be reconciled? What happened?

_____

_____

_____

2. What tendencies do you see in yourself to resist "divine discipline" and correction from others? How might you "get over yourself" so you can benefit from correction?

_____

_____

_____

3. What does Matthew 18:19-20 teach about prayer? What fruit have you seen from praying with others? What can you and at least one other fellow Christian agree on and ask God that it be done today—for the advancement of the kingdom of God here on earth?

_____

_____

_____

Matthew 18:21-35: Forgiveness from the Heart, Without Limit

Only an accountant would look at the parable of the two servants and want to figure out the extent of their debts in work hours. Such a tallying, however, does lead to a startling discovery. One hundred *denarii* represented a laborer's wages for a hundred *days* of work. Ten thousand talents represented wages equivalent to 150,000 *years* of work, more than half a million times greater. The figures highlight the smallness of the second servant's debt in comparison with the first, and they highlight the immensity of the debt the first servant owed to his king!

While the number and nature of our sins may differ, we all sin. When we do, we naturally tend to hide the fact or point to the wrong done to us: "He did this." "She said that." "It's unfair and it hurt me." Jesus knew all too well this tendency in us, and so in teaching us to forgive our brothers and sisters, he first set our sights on a higher reality—God's forgiveness of our sins. Compared to our offenses against God, the debts others owe us seem ridiculously small. Being honest with ourselves, simple justice dictates that we should forgive others without limit.

Consider the words of C. S. Lewis, "To forgive the incessant provocations of daily life—to keep on forgiving the bossy mother-in-law, the bullying husband, the nagging wife, the selfish daughter, the deceitful son—how can we do it? Only, I think, by meaning our words when we say in our prayers each night, 'Forgive us our trespasses as we forgive those that trespass against us.' We are offered forgiveness on no other terms. To refuse to do it is to refuse God's mercy on ourselves" (*The Weight of Glory*, "On Forgiveness").

1. How does Jesus' teaching on forgiveness in this passage relate to the previous passage (Matthew 18:15-20)?

_____

_____

_____

2. Perhaps there are people in your life you have forgiven over and over and who you will, no doubt, have to keep on forgiving. What motivates your forgiveness, and how do you sustain it?

_____

_____

_____

3. When you see God's mercy extended to others, how do you respond? With joy? With jealousy? With resentment? How clearly do you recognize your own need for God's mercy?

_____

_____

_____

Matthew 19:1-12: Upholding the Sanctity of Marriage

Leaving Galilee and returning to the region of Judea, Jesus took another step on the road to his passion and death. In Galilee, he had revealed the power of God in signs, wonders, and clear teachings. In Judea, he would face crafty testing by the Pharisees and scribes. Despite this, he would continue to heal and bring the good news of God's love to the people, and he would continue to form his disciples and invite them to life in him (see Matthew 19:1–22:46).

In one clever test, the Pharisees questioned Jesus on the controversial subject of divorce, hoping to discredit him. Today, especially on the political battlefield, we frequently see how inserting controversial topics into discussions can embroil all sides in heated arguments. Jesus, not taking the bait, set a clear and godly plan for human relationships using Scripture, which the Pharisees could not refute. He referred to the creation story and God's original intent for man and woman that they become inseparably united—"one flesh"—in marriage (Matthew 19:4-6; see also Genesis 2:24).

Marital love and stability require faith and obedience to the Father, who desires to transform our thoughts and actions toward each other through the work of Christ in us. Through personal efforts alone—no matter how emphatic and sincere—we can never attain this high ideal. As followers of Jesus, let us pray for the strength and perseverance to embrace the life of Christ and follow in his footsteps—the way of love and obedience. And let us remember that God is faithful. No matter what our circumstances may be, if we turn to him, he will hear our prayer and show us the way.

1. What hallmarks distinguish self-giving love through faith in Christ from what Jesus described as "hardness of heart" (Matthew 19:8)?

2. What social attacks against marriage are of most concern to you? What action(s) can you take to uphold the sanctity of marriage in society today?

3. How can you strengthen your own marriage and your unity with your spouse? How can you support your married and single friends in following God's ways?

Matthew 19:13-15: Leading Children to Christ

"Let the little children come to me, and do not stop them" (Matthew 19:14). From the time of the patriarchs, Jewish parents always brought their children to the elders of the faith for a blessing. Jesus' disciples, perhaps to save him from what they saw as an annoyance and an interruption of his work, attempted to turn the children away. Once again, Jesus showed that our ways are not his ways. He commanded the apostles to allow the children to come to him.

The new life of God given to each child at baptism requires careful nurturing, in much the same way that a seed needs the right conditions to foster healthy growth. We do damage to a child's faith when we fail to teach him or her about Jesus or when we conduct ourselves as poor examples. We sow confusion in the child's mind when we convey the impression that worldly acclaim and material success take precedence over a relationship with Jesus. If our homes are not places where Jesus is welcomed, the trust that small children may have in the Lord is quickly lost as they mature.

How different the results when we bring our children to Jesus! Our children, entrusted to us by God, respond with joy when Jesus has the opportunity to work within them, "for it is to such as these that the kingdom of heaven belongs" (Matthew 19:14). For this to happen, we have to teach them about Jesus, read the Bible with them, train them in God's ways and the teachings of the church, and attend Mass with them. We must not force "religion" on them but do all we can to win their hearts to Christ. Through our own prayer and example, our sons and daughters will come to desire the life of Christ that they see in us.

1. Reflect on your current attitudes and habits. What area(s) of your life do you wish to change to become more like these kingdom children?

_____

_____

_____

2. Take a walk around your home. In how many ways does it say, "Jesus, you are welcome here"?

_____

_____

_____

3. What have you learned from the faith of children? In what concrete ways might you teach the good news the next time you are surrounded by children?

_____

_____

_____

Matthew 19:16-22: God, Our First Priority

A young man encountering Jesus asked, "What good deed must I do to have eternal life?" He sought some new task, some additional conformity to the law that would ensure his desired end. Perhaps his heart beckoned him to surpass mere observance of the commandments, to which he had been constantly faithful (see Matthew 19:16, 20). Jesus graciously invited him to share in discipleship, which for him would involve voluntarily giving up his great wealth (see 19:21-22).

Following Jesus requires that we detach ourselves from anything that may prevent us from giving ourselves to the service of Christ. This could mean money, career, talents, or social standing—anything that might deter us from making God our first priority.

Dorothy Day, an outspoken twentieth-century Catholic activist, dedicated herself to the care of the poor and the destitute in the fifty Houses of Hospitality that she founded during her lifetime. On poverty and the freedom that comes with it, she wrote, "A readiness for poverty, a disposition to accept it, is enough to begin with. We will always get what we need. 'Take no thought for what you shall eat or drink—the Lord knows you have need of these things'" (*Meditations of Dorothy Day*).

We have all heard the call to follow Jesus. What is our response? Do we believe that as we detach ourselves from the things of this world God will care for us and that the treasure of heaven will fulfill us?

1. Imagine asking Jesus the same question that the rich young man asked (see Matthew 19:16). How do you suppose Jesus would answer you?

_____

_____

_____

2. Consider your belongings, investments, memberships, scheduled events, and routine tasks. What are your attitudes toward them? What do they indicate about your values and priorities? How do they affect your openness to discipleship in Christ?

_____

_____

_____

3. What have you already sacrificed to follow Jesus? What are you willing to give up to more fully pursue discipleship in Christ?

_____

_____

_____

Matthew 19:23-30: God's Rightful Place

Wealth in and of itself is not evil. References to the dangers of wealth in both the Old and New Testaments mainly concern our attitudes toward riches that deny God his proper place of authority (Isaiah 2:7; Proverbs 11:28; 1 John 2:15). Jesus reaffirmed this when he told the disciples about the difficulty the rich have in entering God's kingdom (Matthew 19:24, 28-29).

After hearing Jesus' teaching, the disciples "were greatly astounded and said, 'Then who can be saved?'" (Matthew 19:25). Perhaps we respond with similar anxiety, since the deeper implications of Jesus' warning suggest that any and all practices that seek security from worldly possessions bankrupt our spiritual treasure.

In his desire for our wholehearted love, Jesus invites us to look more closely at our attachment to wealth. He wants us to turn from material pursuits and anxieties about possessions and instead begin to use and distribute the spiritual riches he offers us. Although we readily forget that all we have, all of life, comes to us as a gift from God, we must trust God's promise to provide for our every need. Until we trust in God's divine providence, we will not experience the eternal riches in Christ.

Our attachment to worldly riches may make a spiritual detachment to them seem impossible, but Jesus had the answer: "For mortals it is impossible, but for God all things are possible" (Matthew 19:26). The rewards for those who accept Jesus' invitation surpass comprehension (see 1 Corinthians 2:9). Knowing this truth, we must begin to trust God and act with confidence in his care for us.

1. Why do you think the disciples asked Jesus, "Then who can be saved?" (Matthew 19:25)? Do you assume certain classes or types of people will or will not enter heaven? What did Jesus say?

_____

_____

_____

2. Recall an instance when God performed the impossible in your life. What impact has that had on your faith and trust in God?

_____

_____

_____

3. Peter asked Jesus, "What then will we have?" (Matthew 19:27) in return for leaving everything to follow him. In what ways has Jesus rewarded your discipleship?

_____

_____

_____

Matthew 20:1-16: The Privilege of Serving Christ

Imagine working an entire day for the same pay as a person who worked for only one hour. We would be outraged. Seen through the filter of the world—its concerns and rules of fairness—we readily side with the laborers in this parable who thought that since they had worked longer hours, they should receive more pay. That sounds fair.

We naturally think this way, but in doing so we fail to consider the deeper meaning behind Jesus' parable about the kingdom of God. Fairness isn't the issue. In truth, none of us deserves anything from God. In serving him, we receive much more than we ever give him. Working in the vineyard, in God's kingdom, we receive a great privilege! If we have responded early, we are not unfortunate or ill-used; we are favored.

If we have responded late, we are favored too!

St. Teresa of Avila (1515–1582) expressed it this way: "We should forget the number of years we have served him, for the sum total of all we can do is worthless by comparison with a single drop of the blood which the Lord shed for us. The more we serve him, the more deeply we fall into his debt" (*Life*).

Jesus told this parable of the workers in the vineyard as he journeyed to Jerusalem, where he knew he would be crucified. His death and resurrection transformed the world, filling it with his love. When we know and follow Jesus, when we experience his transforming love, we know the privilege of serving unreservedly in his vineyard.

1. What does this parable suggest to you about God's generosity? About God's justice?

_____

_____

_____

2. How—and why—is the parable of the laborers in the vineyard either comforting or unsettling to you?

_____

_____

_____

3. How do the vineyard owner's actions challenge your ideas of "fairness"? In what ways does this parable alter how you look at serving God?

_____

_____

_____

Matthew 20:17-28: The Cup of Service

Jesus knew that his earthly mission as Savior would come to a climax with his crucifixion. He had spoken several times to the apostles about his journey to Jerusalem and what would happen there (see Matthew 16:21; 17:22-23; 20:17-19), but they didn't understand the meaning of his words. Once again, Jesus calmly and clearly told his disciples details about his death (see 20:28).

Soon after this declaration, the mother of James and John asked Jesus to grant her sons places of honor in his kingdom. Jesus used her request to underscore the essence of the cross. When he asked James and John if they could drink the cup of suffering, and they responded positively, he assured them that they would indeed drink the bitter cup—as servants of Christ (see Matthew 20:23, 26).

Just as the cross was central to Jesus' life, so must it be central to the lives of his followers. The prospect of this may leave us bewildered and fearful, just as Jesus' prediction to his apostles left them wondering whether or not they could endure what lay ahead for them.

St. Teresa of Avila (1515–1582) said that when Jesus asks us, as he asked James and John, if we can drink of his cup, we should reply, "We can." Teresa said that it is "quite right to do so, for his Majesty gives strength to those who, he sees, have need of it, and he defends these souls in every way" (*Interior Castle*, "Sixth Mansions," XI). This promise should fill us with hope and courage in the face of whatever Jesus may demand of us. Through his grace, we can live in obedience to the Father, just as Jesus did.

1. How do you think the disciples reacted to Jesus' clear prophecy of his death? What is the connection between the prophecy and the mother's request?

_____

_____

_____

2. What do you understand the cup of Christ to mean? In light of this passage, how do you feel about drinking this?

_____

_____

_____

3. Why were the other apostles indignant at James and John? How did Jesus address—and correct—their reaction?

_____

_____

_____

Matthew 20:29-34: The Earnest Cry of Faith

A blind beggar alongside the road to Jerusalem was probably quite a familiar sight to the people of Jericho and to the pilgrims—and, unfortunately, one that rarely evoked much attention or sympathy from them. These two beggars, however, though physically blind, had a spiritual perception of Jesus' identity that many of those in the crowd lacked. They shouted to him as he passed by, "Lord, have mercy on us, Son of David!" (Matthew 20:30). And they were not intimidated by efforts to silence them (see 20:31).

Jesus heard and recognized the beggars' earnest cries of faith. He called to them, and they responded eagerly. When the Lord asked what they wanted, they replied, "Lord, let our eyes be opened" (Matthew 20:33). Immediately, touched with pity and compassion, Jesus restored their sight. They threw aside the hopelessness of their old life of begging and followed Jesus (see 20:34).

Like these blind beggars, we need to throw off our old ways. We need renewed energy to respond to Jesus in faith. Burdened by our seeming hopelessness—our patterns of sin, marital problems, family or business difficulties—we have to recognize our need and cry out with faith in Jesus' healing power.

Too often we first try to eliminate hopelessness through our own ingenuity, logic, and wishful thinking. Only when all has failed do we turn to God, who wants us to seek his help and to realize that in the cross of Christ the power resides for us to be filled with new life. By the saving death of Jesus, we have been freed for discipleship. His precious blood has the power to remove whatever may hinder our wholehearted response.

1. Jesus was "moved with compassion" (Matthew 20:34) for the blind beggars. What other emotions do you think Jesus experienced when he met these two? What else do you learn about Jesus by his response to them?

_____

_____

_____

2. What do you learn from the two blind beggars about prayers of petition?

_____

_____

_____

3. When have you prayed loudly and persistently? What was the result? What prayer do you need to pray loudly and persistently today?

_____

_____

_____

Matthew 21:1-11: Jesus' Humble Entry into Jerusalem

Jesus did not enter Jerusalem as a great conquering king mounted on a majestic horse, but as a meek and humble servant, riding an ass, the work beast of the poor. Yet in doing so, he fulfilled the Old Testament prophecy of the triumphant king: "Lo, your king comes to you / . . . humble and riding on a donkey" (Zechariah 9:9).

Though Jesus may not have met the messianic expectations of some, he had clearly made a big impact on large numbers of people. When he entered Jerusalem, he found that "the whole city was in turmoil" (Matthew 21:10). Perhaps the turmoil among the people was due to their great king coming as one of them, not high on a horse above them, but lowly and without pomp.

Jesus is, as Peter confessed, the "Son of the living God" (Matthew 16:16). He is "Lord," but he does not "lord" it over us. He is one of us, living among us. Though he is the king of heaven and earth, the king of glory, he is still approachable. He came not to conquer or oppress, but to free us.

In the incarnation, Christ—the Word of God—became human. Not only did he take "the form of a slave," but he also "humbled himself and became obedient to the point of death—even death on a cross" (Philippians 2:7, 8). He could have come as a great earthly king, seated on a magnificent throne, the object of adoration. Instead, he identified with the lowly and poor. His only moment of glory on earth was this: riding into Jerusalem on an ass. He would go to any lengths to draw us close to him.

1. How would you describe the atmosphere surrounding Jesus' entry into Jerusalem? How did Jesus respond to the crowd? In what ways does the atmosphere help you understand the unfolding events?

   _____

   _____

   _____

2. What do you think an atheist would say about Jesus' entry into Jerusalem? What is your own response to this scene?

   _____

   _____

   _____

3. How is Jesus' entry into Jerusalem like his incarnation? What does this suggest to you about the nature of God?

   _____

   _____

   _____

Matthew 21:12-17: Offering Pleasing Sacrifices to God

Jesus humbled himself and became man to turn the hearts of all people back to God. He willingly accepted this mission because he longed for God to receive the thanks, praise, and worship of those he had created. With this in mind, we can better understand why Jesus became angry at what he saw happening in the temple.

When Jesus entered the temple, he saw traders selling goods for sacrifices. In Jesus' time, sacrifices offered to God at the altar could be bought and sold. This practice, which was regulated by the temple authorities, did not anger Jesus. Rather, it was the hardness of the peoples' hearts that angered him, for they believed this form of worship would satisfy God and fulfill their obligations. To God, however, these attitudes made sacrifices empty actions.

God does not want sacrifices that don't involve our inner conversion. Rather, a sacrifice pleasing to God comes from "a broken and contrite heart" (Psalm 51:17). God wants a people who "maintain justice, and do what is right," who keep "the sabbath, not profaning it" (Isaiah 56:1, 2). He wants people who please him and hold fast to his ways.

Whenever we choose generosity over selfishness or humility over pride, we offer pleasing sacrifices to God. Likewise, when we pursue what the Holy Spirit reveals to us in our prayer times and during our worship services, we please our God. In this way, the temples of our bodies become houses of prayer. "My house shall be called a house of prayer" (Matthew 21:13).

1. What did Jesus indicate about himself by cleansing the temple of the money changers and other sellers? How does this scene affect your image of Jesus?

_____

_____

_____

2. What spiritual conversions have occurred within you recently? Recount these to affirm that indeed the Spirit is at work in you, his "temple" and dwelling place.

_____

_____

_____

3. What action can you perform today that reflects your love for God and for the worship of God?

_____

_____

_____

Matthew 21:18-22: Nurturing a Fruitful Faith

Jesus was hungry. Searching a fig tree for some of its fruit, he found none, and so he dried up the tree (see Matthew 21:18-19). It had failed to bear good fruit. In a similar way, we have been created to know, love, and serve God. The obvious question is, then, "Do we see the good fruit in our lives?" If we keep the Lord and our faith "boxed in"—separate from our everyday lives and thoughts—then we will not bear good fruit. If we place the Lord at the center of our lives and our hearts, however, we will naturally bear good fruit for him.

Jesus told his disciples that if they "have faith and do not doubt" (Matthew 21:21), they could do more than simply wither a fig tree; they could move mountains. According to the *Catechism of the Catholic Church*, "Faith is an entirely free gift that God makes to man. We can lose this priceless gift. . . . To live, grow, and persevere in the faith until the end we must nourish it with the word of God; we must beg the Lord to increase our faith; it must be 'working through charity,' abounding in hope, and rooted in the faith of the Church" (162).

In our journey through this earthly life, we will probably have moments when we feel weak in our faith. When we have moments of doubt, we should ask our Father to strengthen our faith. "Whatever you ask for in prayer with faith, you will receive," Jesus promised (Matthew 21:22). Faith is the soil and nourishment that will allow our lives to become fruitful. If we fail to nurture our faith, we, too, will have little fruit to bear for the Lord.

1. What insights into the power and dynamics of faith do you gain from the story of the fig tree?

_____

_____

_____

2. How does this passage shed light on the meaning of prayer?

_____

_____

_____

3. What can you do to make sure that you allow Christ to remain rooted in the center of your heart? What good fruit do you see springing from your life in Christ?

_____

_____

_____

Matthew 21:23-27: Authority from the Heavenly Father

Two of the most important words or phrases in this passage are "authority" (Matthew 21:23) and "from heaven" (21:25). Both lead us to conclude that the nature of Jesus is divine (from heaven) and that he received his authority to act from the Father, who is in heaven. These concepts help us better understand Jesus and know what our daily responses to him should be.

All of Jesus' authority comes from the Father. Before time began, before creation, Jesus as the Word was present with the Father (see John 1:1). Everything that was created was created through him (see John 1:3; Colossians 1:16). And in his resurrection, Jesus received authority over all that was created. In his own words, "All authority in heaven and on earth has been given to me" (Matthew 28:18). With what reverence and awe should we come into Jesus' presence and acknowledge his holiness! We should tremble at the thought of approaching such holiness.

The Father sent his Son to dwell among us. In an Advent address, Pope John Paul II spoke of the nearness of God to us through his Son: "God has given the greatest testimony of his nearness by sending on earth his Word, the second person of the Most Holy Trinity, who took on a body like ours and came to live among us." The pope also pointed out what our response should be: "With gratitude for this condescension of God who desired to draw near to us . . . by addressing us in the very person of his only begotten Son, we repeat with humble and joyous faith: 'You alone are the Holy One, you alone are the Lord, you alone are the Most High, Jesus Christ, with the Holy Spirit, in the glory of God the Father, Amen.'"

1. Jesus pushed the chief priest and the elders to grasp a larger reality present in his person. What larger reality do you grasp in the presence of Jesus?

_____

_____

_____

2. In what ways do you allow Jesus to exercise his authority over you?

_____

_____

_____

3. Instead of questioning Jesus' authority, how can you affirm it?

_____

_____

_____

Matthew 21:28-32: Responding to God's Will

How many times have we quickly agreed to do something and then failed to follow through? Or how many times have we refused to do something, only to rethink our position later and do it? Both an instant willingness without follow-through and a reluctant accountability can show weakness, a lack of love, and imprecision of purpose.

Combine the yes of the second son with the follow-through of the first, and we have a snapshot of Jesus. He always sought the will of the Father, looked to him for the power to obey, and then faithfully accomplished his tasks. Through his ultimate obedience, the cross, Jesus paved the way for our obedience to the Father as well. We have but to ask and then receive our inheritance of grace as children of God. God created us for this reason; we need not shrink back from it, especially in our more difficult situations—we need only look to Christ. No matter what the situation, God only asks that we do our best without fear of failure or fear of what we might lose. And if we fall short, God graciously calls us to repent and be strengthened.

God our Father deeply desires to help us. Knowing our weaknesses, he continually invites us to turn to him. "Again, when the wicked turn away from the wickedness they have committed and do what is lawful and right, they shall save their life" (Ezekiel 18:27). We have only to be open to God to receive the gift of his love and his help. Let us do what is right by merely accepting in faith the grace of Christ.

1. What point was Jesus making when he told the chief priests and elders that tax collectors and harlots would go into the kingdom of God before them (see Matthew 21:31-32)? Why do you suppose sinners and the socially marginalized respond to Jesus far more quickly than the powerful, wealthy, and wise?

_____

_____

_____

2. Recall an instance when you were reluctant to obey God but then followed through. What motivated you to change your mind?

_____

_____

_____

3. What concrete steps can you take to free yourself to obey God from this day forward?

_____

_____

_____

Matthew 21:33-46: Living in and for Christ

The story of the wicked tenants is an allegory of salvation history. God, the owner of the vineyard—that is, the Jewish nation—placed his people in the care and protection of the religious and political leaders. Their role was to bring the people to fruitfulness through knowing, loving, and obeying God so that they might continue to enjoy his love and protection. From time to time, God sent his prophets to remind the leaders and the people of this purpose; but, they abused, rejected, and even murdered the prophets. Finally, God sent his Son, but the people reviled him, too, and put him to death.

Jesus' mission on earth was to form the church, a new people of God. United by submission and obedience to the Father's will, the church would live out the fullness of God's life and love and would one day enjoy the eternal inheritance promised to all the faithful. As this church, we all too often respond like the tenants of the vineyard, however. We seek the owner's inheritance (see Matthew 21:38); we seek to become our own individual lords and masters. The pride within the human heart spurs us to take control of our lives and find fulfillment apart from God and obedience to him.

Our far more awesome and powerful God earnestly desires that we, the members of his church, commit our lives to his Son and listen to his word in prayer, in Scripture, and in the celebration of the liturgy. For only through Jesus and in union with him do we recognize the voice of the Holy Spirit. As we hear the Spirit's voice and turn to God, we will enjoy the fullness of life in God's kingdom and bear fruit for him.

1. How does this parable point to Jesus' passion? Why, instead of heeding Jesus' warning, did the chief priests and Pharisees want to kill Jesus?

_____

_____

_____

2. When in your life have you acted like the tenants? When have you acted like one who gives the landowner the produce of the harvest? What happened in each situation?

_____

_____

_____

3. In what ways are you giving back to God what God expects of you? What more can you do?

_____

_____

_____

Matthew 22:1-14: Many Are Called, but Few Are Chosen

In his abundant mercy, God invites all people to the royal banquet, the wedding of his Son to the church. The prophet Isaiah announced the Lord's invitation: "On this mountain the LORD of hosts will make for all peoples a feast" (Isaiah 25:6). In the parable of the wedding feast, we again hear of a banquet open to all people, a feast from which no one is excluded (see Matthew 22:1-14).

Isaiah and Jesus both emphasized that the Lord's invitation was not an exclusive, high-society event. God invites everyone, regardless of status in the community, personal history, wealth, race, age, or disability. Isaiah and Jesus both speak of a radical mixing of social groups—just as radical a notion in their times as it is in ours. The Pharisees of Jesus' day, for instance, shunned tax collectors and sinners—but these "sinners" were often the first to accept Jesus (see Matthew 9:10-12). Today, we often see the rich shun the gospel, while the poor embrace it eagerly.

In the Sacrament of the Eucharist, God invites all people to taste his great love. As we participate in the Liturgy of the Eucharist, God increases our desire and readiness for the heavenly banquet still to come. How will we respond to the Lord's invitation to the wedding banquet of his Son? Are we too preoccupied with worldly affairs, or are we prepared to accept the invitation humbly? Jesus said, "For many are called, but few are chosen" (Matthew 22:14). The king rejected the improperly dressed man because the man did not regard his invitation as a great honor. The guests who came dressed in wedding garments recognized God's abundant mercy and love as their only source of strength and hope, and so they "clothed" themselves with this mercy.

1. Why, in your opinion, was the poorly dressed wedding guest treated so severely? What do you think of this treatment? Why?

_____

_____

_____

2. How would you draw an analogy between the parable of the wedding banquet and the call to Christianity made by the church today?

_____

_____

_____

3. What steps have you taken in response to God's invitation? How will you come clothed to the heavenly banquet? What can you do to be well prepared?

_____

_____

_____

Matthew 22:15-22: Performing Christian Political Service

Jesus said, "Give therefore to the emperor the things that are the emperor's, and to God the things that are God's" (Matthew 22:21). All citizens of the empire owed their allegiance to the emperor, but Jesus points out the supreme importance of allegiance to God, for "there is no authority except from God" (Romans 13:1).

As adopted children of our heavenly Father, we are called and chosen to be a holy people, set apart for God's praise and glory (Ephesians 1:4-6). The Father wants us to share his divine life right now, as well as in eternity, to develop an intimate relationship with him, to speak with him in prayer and hear from him through his word.

We have received a privileged citizenship and with it a call to extend God's kingdom on earth.

This is why, even as a people set apart, we need to see the importance of political affairs. The Fathers of the Second Vatican Council taught, "The Church praises and esteems the work of those who for the good of men devote themselves to the service of the state and take on the burdens of this office" (*Pastoral Constitution on the Church in the Modern World*, 75).

As followers of Christ, we have a responsibility to bring an authentic Christian voice to governmental and political affairs. In doing so, we must first and foremost acknowledge God's authority in our lives, and from this starting point pursue the common good, all the while demonstrating our respect for the established civil authority.

1. What do you think are the "things that are God's" (Matthew 22:21)? How do you give God these things and fulfill your obligations to him?

_____

_____

_____

2. How do you think Jesus would respond to the political affairs of our society—apart from siding with either a liberal or conservative agenda?

_____

_____

_____

3. What one political issue can you focus on and offer your time for the Lord? What will you do?

_____

_____

_____

Matthew 22:23-33: The Living Hope of Resurrection

The Sadducees did not believe in the resurrection of the body after death. Thus, when they asked Jesus about the often-married widow of seven brothers (see Matthew 22:28), they intended to entrap him. Jesus seized the opportunity to teach the truth about the resurrection, that when a person rises to eternal life, the laws of earthly life no longer apply. All become like angels, bathed in heavenly life. He admonished them for not knowing the Scriptures or the power of God (see 22:29).

Jesus taught that the resurrection hope has its roots in the character of God. God is a living spirit, faithful to his promises (see Psalm 145:13). God is an all-present and eternal living God who offers us his life (see John 10:10; 1 John 5:11). The Sadducees missed the message of the book of Moses when they pointed to the truth that God is the God of the living, not of the dead (see Matthew 22:32; Exodus 3:6).

What about us? Do we believe in resurrection? Do we believe in the God of life? In order for the resurrection to be a living truth giving us hope, we, too, must know the Scriptures, the living word. This living word affirms in our hearts the truth of the resurrection. If we favor the truth of this world over the truth of Scripture, our hearts will not know the Spirit's teachings about God.

St. Paul wrote, "If the Spirit of him who raised Jesus from the dead dwells in you, he who raised Christ from the dead will give life to your mortal bodies also through his Spirit that dwells in you" (Romans 8:11). The fullness of the resurrection hope can now be known to us through faith, enlightened by the Holy Spirit. This hope is ours now in Christ Jesus.

1. What was it about Jesus and this teaching that "astounded" the crowd (Matthew 22:33)?

_____

_____

_____

2. How does Jesus' teaching in Matthew 22:31-32 affect your faith in resurrection to new life? How can you share this faith with others?

_____

_____

_____

3. Swap out the names Abraham, Isaac, and Jacob in Matthew 22:32 for some of your favorite saints' names. How does this change or enhance your expectations for resurrected life?

_____

_____

_____

Matthew 22:34-40: The Law of Love

When the Pharisees asked Jesus which commandment was the greatest, they expected him to describe the most essential aspect of the law. Jesus' answer—love of God, first, and love of neighbor because of this—centered all observance of the law on love. Jesus stressed the point that the righteousness of every word and deed within human life depends on love.

St. Paul understood this: "Love is the fulfilling of the law" (Romans 13:10). The Father demonstrated love by sending his only Son to bring us forgiveness and to reconcile us with the Father. Jesus, who is God's "love calling us to love in return" (Abbot William of St. Thierry, *The Contemplation of God*), said yes to the Father's plan, out of love for him and for us. We enter into and experience this same love when we unite ourselves to God's will in Christ Jesus.

How do we love, then? Unlike the popular notions of love that we learn from television, movies, magazines, and books, love of God means that we worship him only, not our families, jobs, or possessions. It means willing ourselves to do what God wants us to do. We receive the power to do this by his love for us. That, and not just a wonderful tingly feeling inside, is love of God.

To love our neighbors means that we treat them and respond to them with patience and kindness and that we "[bear] all things" (1 Corinthians 13:4, 7). We may accomplish this only when our love of neighbor has its roots in love of God—and only then will our words and actions bear fruit for the salvation of others. The power comes from God—but the decision to respond is ours.

1. What do you think the lawyer hoped to achieve by testing Jesus? How do you suppose the lawyer reacted to Jesus' answer?

   _____

   _____

   _____

2. Why did Jesus teach us to love God first? How is that more important than loving our neighbors first?

   _____

   _____

   _____

3. What does the second commandment require of us? Think of a person whom you find challenging to love. Try focusing all your strength on loving God, and then see what happens to your love for this person.

   _____

   _____

   _____

Matthew 22:41-46: The Lordship of the Son of David

The Davidic "sonship" of the Messiah had firm grounding in Hebrew Scripture (see Isaiah 9:2-7; 2 Samuel 7:11-14). Additionally, the Holy Spirit had revealed to David that the Messiah was not only the "son of David" but David's Lord (see Matthew 22:44; Psalm 110:1). Thus, Jesus' challenge was to show that not only was he the son of David, the long-awaited Messiah, but also that he came not simply to extend a political Davidic dynasty but to inaugurate the kingdom of God.

How can we know the truth of Jesus' teachings? How can we know that Jesus is indeed "true God from true God"? How can we know that the Holy Spirit issues from the Father and the Son? How can we know that Christ established the church? We can only know the truth of these things by asking the Holy Spirit to reveal them to us. This is especially true of Jesus' identity as our Lord and Savior: "The Holy Spirit, whom the Father will send in my name, will teach you everything, and remind you of all that I have said to you" (John 14:26). We must avoid the thinking and the pathway that pursues answers to these questions through the intellect or the emotions alone.

As we pray and study Scripture, the Holy Spirit will inspire us with knowledge and revelation. Have faith and believe the truths that the church proclaims at the heart of her faith. With this as the starting point, the Spirit furthers our spiritual and intellectual understanding. St. Augustine said, "I do not seek to understand in order to believe; I believe in order to understand." In these days of relativism and uncertainty, we must trust (lean on) the Spirit to teach us the awesome truths of the faith. As we stand firm in our faith in Christ, the Spirit will lead us to deeper understanding.

1. Jesus' questions and answers silenced (and angered) some of the most brilliant men of his day. What does this imply about the role of reason in your relationship with God?

_____

_____

_____

2. Do you seek to understand in order to believe? Or do you believe in order to understand? Explain your answer.

_____

_____

_____

3. Have you ever had to trust Jesus, despite your lack of understanding, and then continue to pray, attend Mass, and perform works of mercy? How did this affect your faith?

_____

_____

_____

Matthew 23:1-12: Abandoning Self to Serve Others

The scribes and Pharisees did God's work when they preached and taught in the synagogues, but in doing so they also consciously drew attention to themselves. "They do all their deeds to be seen by others" (Matthew 23:5). They sought places of honor at feasts, the best seats in the synagogues, and reverent titles to puff up their egos (see 23:6-7). They fell victim to pride and vanity.

We naturally want to draw attention to ourselves—we want glory. Perhaps because of our fallen nature, we enjoy being at the center of things when we have done a laudable deed. Jesus reminds us that when doing his work, we must serve. We must wash the feet of others (see John 13:14-15)—not expect others to wash our feet. The "greatest" of disciples must possess a servant's heart (see Matthew 23:11). The motivation for serving Christ must be love for others, not glory for self.

Although contrary to our baser instincts, what we need is a willingness to forget ourselves. Our purest moments of love are those in which we let go of our vision of ourselves and focus on the needs of others. This disposition of self-abandonment allows us to draw closer to the Lord, to be caught up in his love and goodness. When we serve others, we imitate our Lord Jesus. He who was truly the greatest among us was also the servant who washed the feet of his disciples.

When we find ourselves consumed by prideful attitudes, we need to repent and ask the Lord to help us serve as he served. The more we become aware of our prideful tendencies, the more we can rise above them, with God's grace.

1. Jesus, the Messiah, implied that he is the servant of all (see Matthew 23:10-11). What does this teach you about your role in the world as a Christian—a follower of Christ?

_____

_____

_____

2. In what situations have you grown accustomed to being served? In what meaningful and sensible ways could you turn the tables and become the servant in those situations?

_____

_____

_____

3. What "feeds" your pride? What motivates you to be humble and to serve?

_____

_____

_____

Matthew 23:13-36: The Woes of Injustice and Unrighteousness

Why would Jesus choose to rebuke the scribes and Pharisees, the religious leaders of his day? He recognized in them a tendency to use religion to suit their own purposes, to exalt themselves, and to ultimately reject true faith. He confronted these sins in them, because—if left unchecked—their sins would lead them to spiritual death. Jesus grieved over their condition and pronounced a series of woes, clear warnings of the unhappy consequences of their behavior.

In the first two woes, Jesus accused the scribes and Pharisees of hindering people from entering the kingdom of God (see Matthew 23:13, 15). Not only did the religious leaders choose not to enter themselves, but they also blocked the way for others by their rejection of Christ. He also pointed out their hypocrisy in claiming to lead people to God but failing to encourage true holiness, not just religiosity. Finally, Jesus called the Pharisees and scribes "blind guides," because they could not see the truth regarding oath taking (see 23:16). This woe echoes the beatitude forbidding the making of oaths and encouraging his followers to live honest and pure lives (see 5:33-37).

Jesus modeled his woes on Isaiah (5:8-23), who declared the ruin of those who through greed and falsehood distorted true justice and righteousness. Matthew included this passage in his gospel to warn the early Christian community against similar tendencies among themselves. We, too, can take these words as a warning in light of our own situations. Let us ask the Holy Spirit, the Spirit of truth, to show us how we may have distorted the gospel to meet our own needs.

1. What—and how—do the woes add to your understanding of the law and of the "weightier matters of the law: justice and mercy and faith" (Matthew 23:23)?

_____

_____

_____

2. How do you practice what you preach; that is, in what ways is your Christian faith *lived* rather than simply verbalized now and then?

_____

_____

_____

3. Who is your patron saint? In what ways can you emulate this person? How would this be an example of living faith?

_____

_____

_____

Matthew 23:37-39: Crucifixion: The Road of Salvation

At several moments in Matthew's gospel, Jesus predicted his coming passion, death, and resurrection, even at a great distance from Jerusalem (see Matthew 16:21; 17:22-23; 20:17-19). God saw that his people had turned away from his love and, as a result, had fallen into every kind of sin. And Jesus knew that without his death on the cross, the people would end up desolate, separated from the Father's love and protection. Jesus accepted his death because he understood God's plan of redemption and wanted to obey it.

Jesus chose to become flesh in order to take upon himself the punishment that our sins deserved. He recognized the road to Jerusalem and the ascent to Calvary as part of his mission. He knew that his work of reconciling sinners to God would only be accomplished through his death and resurrection. Jesus loved us too much to shrink back from this difficult calling. And even though he was quite aware that Jerusalem had been the death of many a prophet before him (see Matthew 23:37), he was determined to destroy sin in order to finally gather his people in his arms.

Jesus' work of healings and miracles was important, but his atoning sacrificial death was the only way that God's plan to save humanity would be fulfilled. Jesus did not just endure the cross; he chose it freely as the Father's plan for him. He embraced it out of love, moving forward steadily toward Jerusalem because it meant life for God's people. By the blood Jesus shed on the cross, he opened for us the way to the Father.

1. If you could imagine yourself among those listening to Jesus, what would his lament over Jerusalem say to you about his identity? What does Matthew 23:39 add to your understanding of who Jesus is?

   _____

   _____

   _____

2. How does the warning of desolation (see Matthew 23:38) affect your desire to deepen your Christian faith and to love and worship God?

   _____

   _____

3. What desolation has sin brought into your life? What has obedience to Christ and righteousness brought? How do you allow Christ to "gather" you to himself as "a hen gathers her brood under her wings" (Matthew 23:37)?

   _____

   _____

Matthew 24:1-35: The Coming Day of the Lord

People of every age have pondered the end of time, wondering when it would come and what signs would precede it. During the Old Testament period, prophets foretold the coming of the "day of the Lord," when humanity would witness the triumph of God over his enemies. In the New Testament period, the disciples were especially interested in Jesus' prediction of the destruction of the temple in Jerusalem (see Matthew 24:2), which actually occurred in A.D. 70, while many of them were still alive.

One day, Jesus will return (see Matthew 24:30; Acts 1:11). He will return as the Son of Man, unmistakable and visible to all. His coming will be sudden and unexpected (see 1 Thessalonians 5:2-3) and will usher in a new heaven and a new earth. A series of disorders will portend the final days, including the appearance of impostors, times of political upheaval, and the occurrence of natural disasters (see Matthew 24:3-14). And the end will not come until there first has been a time of witnessing and persecution of the church (see Luke 21:12-19).

Each day that the Lord gives us, we should anticipate the coming of Christ. As we go about our daily tasks, even the most mundane ones, we can look forward to the joy that will be ours when Jesus comes to take us home. If we remain faithful to the Lord each day, we need not fear his coming: we are his. Our faith must rest in the promise of eternal life that was made to those who believe in him.

1. In Matthew 24:25 Jesus says, "I have told you beforehand." Why do you suppose Jesus sent us this warning? Does it help you, encourage you, mystify you? What will you do about it?

_____

_____

_____

2. What impact does Jesus' promise that he will return have on the way you live?

_____

_____

_____

3. How prepared are you to face persecution for your faith? Does the knowledge that you are not alone in this struggle encourage you? How so?

_____

_____

_____

Matthew 24:36-44: Preparing Our Hearts for Union with God

As throngs of worshippers made their way toward the temple in Jerusalem, it was customary to sing, "I was glad when they said to me, 'Let us go to the house of the LORD!'" (Psalm 122:1). But Jesus' somewhat ominous prophecy seems almost contradictory to that sense of joy: "Then two will be in the field; one will be taken and one will be left. . . . Keep awake therefore, for you do not know on what day your Lord is coming" (Matthew 24:40, 42).

Inspired by the Holy Spirit, the prophet Isaiah foresaw how these disparate themes of judgment and joy would one day be reconciled, when "many peoples shall come" to God's holy city "that he may teach us his ways and that we may walk in his paths" (Isaiah 2:3). This divine intervention will one day result in a profound peace, such as the world has never known: "Nation shall not lift up sword against nation, neither shall they learn war any more" (2:4).

Jesus inaugurated what Isaiah prophesied; we have a foretaste of the promise now but will know it in its fullness when Jesus comes again in glory. We can prepare our hearts in anticipation of a closer union with God, both now and in the future. We make ready the way of the Lord, not out of fear, but because, in the deepest part of our being, we long to "walk in the light of the LORD" (Isaiah 2:5). Thus, Jesus warned us of the necessary judgment: "Be ready, for the Son of Man is coming at an unexpected hour" (Matthew 24:44). We prepare now in joy, for the day approaches when our preparations and labor will end. Like the psalmist, we, too, will sing for joy as we wait to meet our God.

1. What does Matthew 24:36 suggest to you about Jesus' relationship with his Father?

_____

_____

_____

2. What distracts you from being alert and vigilant for Christ's coming? What daily routines or spiritual practices could help you be better prepared for Christ's return?

_____

_____

_____

3. How can you help spread the necessity for watchfulness in a loving and compassionate way?

_____

_____

_____

Matthew 24:45-51: The Vigilance of the Faithful Servant

Jesus' discourse concerning the end times challenges us to prepare for his return. To ignore his warning by living a self-centered, pleasure-seeking life would be most unwise. Jesus' message here, reminiscent of the challenge expressed earlier (see Matthew 7:24-26), reminds us to build our house on the rock of his words, or we will see it fall. Thus, both at the beginning of his public ministry and as it drew to a close, Jesus put forth the same challenge and the same warning—repent from our sins, listen to God's word, and trust in God who alone saves us, or perish.

Such words of caution are not restricted to the New Testament; they occur throughout the Old Testament as well (in Psalm 1, for example). But this time, Jesus expresses them in the context of his return to Jerusalem, when he will usher in the fullness of the kingdom of God.

As we read of the impending judgments in Jesus' discourse about the end times, we tend to think of ourselves as the "good guys." Few of us would identify ourselves with the wicked (see Matthew 24:48-49). We might do ourselves some good, however, to admit honestly that we sometimes act like the good slave, and sometimes like the wicked one.

Left to our own initiatives, we will not likely remain alert and on guard. Our sins will soon overwhelm us. Thanks to Christ's death and resurrection, however, we can open our lives to God's grace and daily learn to rely on his free gift—not on ourselves. Alertness born from this sure hope in his second coming will abundantly bless us.

1. Name at least three characteristics of the faithful slave in Matthew 24:45-51. How does he or she contrast with the unfaithful slave?

   _____

   _____

   _____

2. What work or duties has the Master entrusted to you?

   _____

   _____

   _____

3. During what times or in what aspects of your life are you least like the faithful slave? How can you change this?

   _____

   _____

   _____

Matthew 25:1-13: The Readiness of the Wise

"Keep awake therefore, for you know neither the day nor the hour" (Matthew 25:13). With these words from the parable of the ten bridesmaids, Jesus once again advises his followers to prepare for his return. Are we like the five wise bridesmaids who prepared flasks of oil for their lamps in anticipation of a great wedding feast? Or are we like the five foolish bridesmaids who took no oil with them and consequently missed their opportunity to enter the banquet hall?

Because we live at such a frenetic pace today, we seldom take the time to reflect on one of God's wonderful promises to us as his sons and daughters—Jesus' return in glory at the end of time. If we ponder Christ's return at all, we tend to focus our thoughts on the timing of his return, and not on the new life that awaits his faithful people or on our preparedness to welcome him.

Scripture encourages us not to obsess about the end of time, when exactly it will occur, and so on. If we stand on our belief that we have been baptized into Jesus' death and resurrection, we can live full of resurrection hope. We can comfort one another with the truth that God wants to raise us all with Christ so that we will always be with the Lord (see 1 Thessalonians 4:17).

When we receive Jesus in the Eucharist, we can ask God to give us great expectation and a vibrant hope in his return. As we proclaim Jesus' death until his return in glory, we can ask the Holy Spirit to fill us with his presence, with the "oil of gladness" as we eagerly await the resurrection—the wedding feast of Jesus and his church.

1. What do you think the lamp oil symbolizes (see Matthew 25:3, 8)? Do you have this "oil" in your possession?

_____

_____

_____

2. How do the five wise bridesmaids reflect your concept of prudence? Of preparedness? What do you need in order to remain in a state of constant readiness for the Lord's return?

_____

_____

_____

3. Do you resemble or identify with the foolish bridesmaids in any way? If so, how can you better prepare to receive the bridegroom?

_____

_____

_____

Matthew 25:14-30: Investing in Spiritual Prosperity

We don't know exactly when or how Jesus will return, we just know that he *will* return in glory to establish a new heaven and a new earth. Therefore, just as an industrious wife takes the initiative in caring for her household (see Proverbs 31:10-31), we must use the church's resources to spread the gospel and to ensure the spiritual prosperity of all people. By walking as "children of light and children of the day"—through obedience to God's commands and a life of prayer and love—we attest to our faith in Christ's return (1 Thessalonians 5:5).

As the parable of the talents shows, two servants took risks with the money they had received, investing it and earning good returns. The third, afraid to take any risks, hid his master's money and returned it at the first opportunity (see Matthew 25:14-30). Like the first two servants, we must take risks for the kingdom of God, putting our faith to work for God's spiritual interests.

God does not give us gifts and talents only to have us hide them or turn them to selfish ends. Every one of us has been uniquely constituted to play a role in the advancement of his kingdom. Whether it be our money, abilities, time, or training and background, we can be assured that our initiatives to use these gifts will be blessed.

As we give of ourselves, we will see God's power and glory revealed. Life is truly an adventure, filled with opportunities to use all that God has given us and to see him work wonders in and through us. This is our high calling. Let us accept it with gratitude and joy.

1. How does the investment of talents compare and contrast with the possession of lamp oil from the previous parable (Matthew 25:1-13)?

   _____

   _____

   _____

2. How would a deeper knowledge of your God-given talents and gifts help you invest yourself more in God's interests?

   _____

   _____

   _____

3. Do you have any "talents" you could unearth and reinvest while there's still time? What are they, and how will you invest them?

   _____

   _____

   _____

Matthew 25:31-46: God's Blessings on the Sheepfold

When we read this parable, we naturally think of the "sheep"—the righteous ones—as wonderful people indeed, giving of themselves for others. Truly, we feel, they deserve the eternal reward awaiting them. But Jesus was driving at a deeper meaning behind the story. He addressed the sheep as "blessed by my Father" (Matthew 25:34). This phrase brings to the forefront a difference between the sheep and the goats. The sheep sought the Father in faith and received his blessing through their care and compassion for the needy in their midst. The goats did no such thing.

Thus, this parable highlights the bountiful gifts of faith—the "sheep" not only did good deeds but they did them as expressions of their faith in God. Because God has made himself known to us and we have faith in him, we are able to move beyond our self-centered concerns to love and care for the sick, the imprisoned, the hungry, and the naked. When we are open to God, trust in God, lean on God and not ourselves, God enters our hearts and provides for all our needs to do his work—and blesses us in doing it.

"Goats" are far more concerned with their own welfare. They are preoccupied with their own status and prestige, their own success—and therefore do not see with the eyes of faith. God wants us to turn to him, to know that he reveals himself to everyone who seeks him sincerely (see Hebrews 11:6). And only through faith in God (which draws us to his love) can we then effectively reach out to others. When we try to do this through our own goodness or willpower, we become like dry springs from which no life can flow to others. If, on the other hand, we ground ourselves in God's love and salvation, God enables us to give and serve selflessly.

1. How would you characterize the "sheep" in your own words? How about the "goats"?

_____

_____

_____

2. How does this passage change the way you think about how to best love God?

_____

_____

_____

3. Which of the corporal works of mercy (see Matthew 25:35-36) do you frequently perform? What is your chief motivation for doing them? If you don't perform any regularly, what plans will you put in place to faithfully perform these tasks?

_____

_____

_____

Matthew 26:1–27:66: The Passion of Christ

Gregory Roa

Gregory Roa is a graduate of the School of Theology and Religious Studies at the Catholic University of America. He lives near Washington, DC, with his wife and four children.

Let us imagine for a moment a non-Christian reading the Gospel of Matthew for the very first time. Not knowing anything about Christianity, he or she would soon notice an odd thing. More details have been supplied about Jesus' final hours than about any other event in his life. We can easily imagine this person asking, "What is so significant about this Jesus' death? Why would it overshadow all the good things he said and did during his life?"

The Gospel of Matthew was not written in a vacuum; it grew out of a community of believers seeking to deepen their faith and love for Jesus, whose death and resurrection had transformed their lives. Consequently, while the gospel does reveal the importance of Jesus' sayings and miracles, it maintains a primary focus on his passion, crucifixion, and death, because in these events the community saw the principal work of their salvation. Without Jesus' cross, all his words and deeds lose their full power and meaning.

Matthew's Focus. This broad, overarching theme of Jesus' cross and resurrection serves as the keystone of Matthew's narrative. Matthew wrote for a Jewish community that had converted to Christianity; and, like all Jews in the late first century, these Jewish Christians keenly felt the impact of the dramatic events of their time—the destruction of the temple and the continuing Roman occupation in their homeland.

Yet these new Christian converts in Matthew's community felt doubly outcast: they were also being driven out of the Jewish synagogues for their belief in Jesus.

The pain of rejection was only part of the struggle of Matthew's community. Their own newly born church was witnessing an influx of non-Jewish converts. For the first time, Jews found themselves worshipping and living alongside Gentiles who accepted the gospel but knew little or nothing about the Torah. The pressure to accept this new reality must have been great.

Besieged by outside forces and strained with tension from within, Matthew's community was in upheaval. From within this context Matthew proclaimed the word of truth, speaking of things that were important to his audience's circumstances. By examining some key elements in Matthew's passion narrative, we can appreciate the community for which Matthew wrote and gain a deeper understanding of Jesus' victory on the cross as it applies to our lives today.

Fulfilling God's Promises. From the outset, Matthew's passion narrative reveals Jesus as a Messiah who remains in control of the events leading to his arrest and death. Matthew begins his story with a matter-of-fact declaration by Jesus: "You know that after two days the Passover is coming, and the Son of Man will be handed over to be crucified" (Matthew 26:2). The tone was set: Jesus would face a difficult trial, but he would embrace the struggle decisively, confident that he was doing his Father's will.

From this point on, Matthew showed Jesus as the obedient Son of God, fulfilling his Father's plan in all things. Just as Jesus had earlier told John the Baptist that he must "fulfill all righteousness" (Matthew 3:15), so here, at the end of his ministry, Jesus fulfilled God's will, moving forward readily to his trial and death. In this way, Matthew showed Jesus living out the teaching he gave his disciples: "But strive first for the kingdom of God and his righteousness" (6:33). Ever faithful to God, Jesus showed himself to be the "Son, the Beloved" with whom his Father was "well pleased" (3:17).

For Matthew, Jesus' radical obedience to God revealed him to be the true and long-awaited Messiah. Immediately after recounting Jesus' passion prediction, Matthew tells of his anointing at Bethany (see Matthew 26:6-13). The Greek word *Christos* means "the anointed one," and though the disciples protested the exorbitant waste of precious oil, Jesus accepted it as a "good service" (26:10), which prepared him "for burial" (26:12). It is significant that a woman, not one of his own disciples, anointed Jesus. Though the Jews were God's chosen people, they had failed to recognize the Messiah in their midst. In contrast, the Gentiles, "sinners," and women—outsiders like those gaining prominence in Matthew's community—rushed to accept him as Savior. For Jesus, discipleship did not depend on gender, background, or race. True disciples are those who, like the anonymous woman at Bethany, have faith in Jesus and do the will of God (see 12:50).

Throughout his passion narrative, Matthew leads us through scriptural allusions and prophecies fulfilled by Jesus' death—all signs of Jesus' obedience to his Father's plan. As you read through Matthew's passion narrative, see how many of these Old Testament parallels you can find: Psalm 2:1-2; Psalm 22; Psalm 41:9; Isaiah 53:3, 7; Jeremiah 32:6-9; Zechariah 11:12-13; 13:7. So much did Matthew rely on the Hebrew Scriptures to explain why Jesus had to die that even Jesus' final words are a direct quote: "Eli, Eli, lema sabachthani?" that is, "My God, my God, why have you forsaken me?" (Matthew 27:46; see Psalm 22:1).

Embracing the "Hour" of the Cross. By using so many scriptural allusions, Matthew was able to accomplish two major goals. First, he could reassure the Jewish Christians that Jesus truly had to die to fulfill the Father's plan for us; the Messiah *had* to be rejected in order to save his people. Second, and more significant, the scriptural parallels reveal that, despite the upheaval, chaos, and pain of the passion, God was, in fact, in control throughout these awful events. When Jesus proclaimed, "My time is near; I will keep the passover" (Matthew 26:18), Matthew used the Greek term *kairos*, meaning "hour" or "moment." Jesus repeated this at Gethsemane when he was arrested: "See, the hour is at hand" (26:45). However it may have appeared to the chief priests and scribes, Jesus decisively embraced the passion as the very moment for which he had been preparing his whole life.

Jesus' suffering was no "accident" or "twist of fate." It was not even the by-product of the chief priests' opposition, Judas' betrayal, or Pilate's power. Jesus' death was God's will for the salvation of all humankind. Still, Matthew made no attempt to hide the emotional turmoil this decision caused Jesus. In fact, he depicted the real, human sorrow and anguish evident when Jesus prayed: "My Father, if it is possible, let this cup pass from me" (Matthew 26:39).

Jesus did not shrink back from the anguish of his cross. He endured it to win our salvation. Now, Matthew's community, undergoing upheaval and suffering, was also encouraged to follow the way of the cross. Despite appearances, God was still in control over history, even over the oppression and tension they were experiencing. It was just as Jesus had promised them: "If any want to become my followers, let them deny themselves and take up their cross and follow me. For those who want to save their life will lose it, and those who lose their life for my sake will find it" (Matthew 16:24-25).

Inaugurating a New World. For the Christian Jews and Gentile converts in Matthew's community, Jesus' coming "to fulfill" the "law [and] the prophets" (Matthew 5:17) meant the dynamic arrival of a new stage of history. Like a new Moses, Jesus had already superseded the law and the prophets in his Sermon on the Mount (see 5:1–7:29). Now, at the Last Supper, he instituted a new covenant, which more than surpassed Israel's former relationship with Yahweh. Matthew depicted this meal as a Passover *seder*, evoking a rich imagery for his Jewish readers. Employing the same symbols the Jews had used since Moses' time, Jesus did more than recall Israel's redemption from slavery. He *transformed* the ceremony, saying, "Take, eat; this is my body. . . . For this is my blood of the covenant, which is poured out for many for the forgiveness of sins" (26:26, 28). The Son of God sacrificed his body and blood to create a new Israel, a church that included Jews and Gentiles, women and men, and every marginalized soul who appears in various places in Matthew's gospel. Through Christ, all now have access to Jesus' *Abba*—our Father.

At the end of the Last Supper, Jesus told his disciples, "I will never again drink of this fruit of the vine until that day when I drink it new with you in my Father's kingdom" (Matthew 26:29). This statement—which is probably as close to the exact words of Jesus as any saying we find in the gospels—indicates again Jesus' awareness of his fate and his willingness to move forward to the victory he would achieve in the cross. It also made Matthew's readers aware that they could no longer look back to the Mosaic laws and rituals from which they came. Because Jesus' time had come, all Christians could now drink the wine of the new covenant, a wine that could not be contained by the old wineskins (see 9:17).

This new stage of history began at the very moment of Jesus' death, as Matthew showed with the events that occurred immediately thereafter:

> From noon on, darkness came over the whole land. . . . Then Jesus cried again with a loud voice and breathed his last. At that moment the curtain of the temple was torn in two, from top to bottom. The earth shook, and the rocks were split. The tombs also were opened, and many bodies of the saints who had fallen asleep were raised. . . . Now when the centurion and those with him, who were keeping watch over Jesus, saw the earthquake and what took place, they were terrified and said, "Truly this man was God's Son!" (Matthew 27:45, 50-52, 54)

Jesus' death accomplished the very thing that Judaism looked for in the coming of the Messiah: the new era of the reign of God, when he promised to shake the earth and raise up his holy ones. Our salvation and renewal began when Jesus died on the cross. Yet God's chosen people—even Jesus' own disciples—missed its inauguration. Once again, it was a group of outsiders, the Roman soldiers, who readily accepted the cross and the signs of transformation that accompanied it.

Hope and Challenge. By telling the story of Jesus' death and resurrection as he did, Matthew sought to hold out hope to a community undergoing enormous pressures from inside and out. On a personal level, we all experience struggles: the pain of rejection, the challenge to do God's will in the face of opposition, the sorrow of apparent failures that face us every day. Like Matthew's community, we, too, can learn that not every obstacle comes from outside of ourselves: "The spirit indeed is willing, but the flesh is weak" (Matthew 26:41). Growth and renewal come at a price: opening ourselves to be shaken up and allowing the Spirit to breathe life into us.

The message of the passion is that Jesus is with us in this process of the upheaval of our old life. Matthew's term for earthquake—*seismos*—was the same word he used when Jesus saved the disciples by calming the *seismos* ("great storm") on the lake (see Matthew 8:23-27). Jesus remains with us, in control of our history, just as he was on the lake and during the distressing events of the passion. While it is a challenge to follow the way of the cross, it is, at the same time, our best hope. If we understand anything from praying through Matthew's narrative, it is that Jesus has already won the victory. We do not see its fullness, but neither could Jesus' disciples—or Matthew's community. Let us be confident that we walk in the new day of God's righteousness and that, with those who persevere with joy, we will "see the Son of Man seated at the right hand of Power / and coming on the clouds of heaven" (26:64).

1. What three adjectives best describe Jesus during the anointing at Bethany (Matthew 26:6-13)? What does your short list of adjectives reveal about Jesus' character and identity? What steps can you take to nurture these character traits in your own life?

_____

_____

_____

2. What parallels do you find between Matthew's passion narrative and the following Scripture passages: Psalm 2:1-2; Psalm 22; Psalm 41:9; Isaiah 53:3, 7; Jeremiah 32:6-9; and Zechariah 11:12-13; 13:7? Which parallels struck you as most significant? Why? Why do you think Matthew used so many Old Testament passages in his gospel (see "Embracing the 'Hour' of the Cross" in the above meditation)?

_____

_____

_____

3. What does Jesus' use of the Greek word *kairos*, meaning "hour" or "moment," in Matthew 26:18, 45, suggest about his foreknowledge of the Father's plan for our salvation? About his trust in the Father?

_____

_____

_____

4. Throughout the passion narrative, Jesus faced the unfolding events with incredible courage. In what ways does his courage strengthen your own faith in God's promises and encourage you to seek your place in his heavenly kingdom?

_____

_____

_____

5. Arguably one of the most emotional scenes of Matthew's passion narrative occurs when Jesus prays in Gethsemane, "My Father, if it is possible, let this cup pass from me" (Matthew 26:39). What does this moment of intense human suffering in Jesus' life help you realize about God's love for you?

_____

_____

_____

7. Sometimes we recognize God's hand in the events of our lives, like the centurion who witnessed Jesus' death and said, "Truly this man was God's Son!" (Matthew 27:54). At other times, we miss it completely, like the Pharisees' frequent failure to truly see or hear Jesus' good news. In your mind, what accounts for the differences between those who hear God and those who don't? Between those who respond to God and those who don't?

_____

_____

_____

8. What relevance do Jesus' passion and death have for your life today? In what ways do you understand yourself to be participating in them this very day?

_____

_____

_____

Matthew 28:1-15: Kingdom Courage Overcomes Fear and Death

At dawn on the first day of the week, two women came to the tomb to pay their last respects to the teacher who had changed their lives. What started as a pious excursion soon became something far more extraordinary. God's presence became evident to them—Matthew reports the occurrence of an earthquake and then the appearance of an angel who rolled back the stone from in front of Jesus' tomb (see Matthew 28:2). The angel instructed the women to tell the apostles what they had seen and heard. Afraid, yet filled with joy (see 28:8), the women ran to proclaim Jesus' resurrection from the dead to the disciples.

The women experienced fear, in part because they had been told to proclaim a truth that they knew might be rejected—it was incredible! Their response was not unlike our own when we experience the wonder of God, but are hesitant to speak of it for fear of what people might think. The women carried out the angel's instruction with joy, however, because the wonder of God at work in them far surpassed their fear.

Despite the fact that the Jewish priests and elders had concocted a story to explain away the resurrection of Jesus (see Matthew 28:12-15), God had a better plan, and the two women were part of it. The testimony of the two Marys—and of all the other witnesses to the truth of Jesus— won the day. Christianity outlived the Roman Empire—and every empire since—all because witnesses to the truth, like these two women, have responded to God and faithfully proclaimed what they have seen. The power of the gospel outlives all the powers the world will ever muster.

1. What stark contrasts do you note between the reaction of the women and the reaction of the chief priests? Where and in what ways do you continue to see these differing reactions today?

_____

_____

_____

2. What impact does your belief in Jesus' resurrection have on your daily life? What has your faith in the risen Lord emboldened you to do?

_____

_____

_____

3. Who has proclaimed the faith to you? Who do you look to as an example of Christian courage? Ask the Spirit to help you emulate the actions of these individuals.

_____

_____

_____

Matthew 28:16-20: The Great Commission

"Go therefore and make disciples of all nations, baptizing them in the name of the Father and of the Son and of the Holy Spirit." (Matthew 28:19). These words have come to be known as the Great Commission. We view them as Jesus' final "marching orders" to the eleven disciples who had been his companions over the preceding three years. Fortunately for us, with the grace of the Holy Spirit upon them, they ably carried out this commission—with exquisite zeal.

But these words do not apply solely to the eleven disciples standing on the mountain. Christianity has flourished through two millennia because others have taken up the great commission. Now we, too, receive Jesus' command to "make disciples of all nations."

What a daunting task! How often we shrink from it, fearful of offending someone or embarrassing ourselves. Yet Jesus ends his commission with these comforting words: "I am with you always, to the end of the age" (Matthew 28:20). As we carry out his commission, Jesus helps us overcome fear, pride, and anything else that deters us from preaching his word.

Through baptism, Jesus lives in us. He who died for us has given us new life, and we can rejoice now and in heaven when we share that life with others. To do this, we can feed the hungry, comfort the lonely, visit the sick. We can work to correct injustice in our societies. We can build strong, loving families. We can invite people to our churches. In all these ways, we build God's kingdom on earth.

1. In what way do the verbs used in Matthew 28:19-20 summarize the mission of the church? Would you add any verbs—for example, from the works of mercy (see Matthew 25:35-36)? Others?

_____

_____

_____

2. In what situations are you most aware of the presence of Christ as he promised, "I am with you always" (Matthew 28:20)? How is Christ present?

_____

_____

_____

3. What are you doing in response to Jesus' commission in Matthew 28:19-20? What, if anything, holds you back from carrying out this command? Consider posting the Great Commission somewhere you frequently look as a reminder of your awesome calling.

_____

_____

_____

APPENDIX 1

Index of Meditations

Plan			Passage	Theme	Page
			1:1-17	God's Extraordinary Plan	25
1			1:18-25	Obedient and Dedicated Faith	26
	3		2:1-12	Gifts for the King	27
			2:13-23	Joseph, the Father Figure	28
		4	3:1-12	Repentance and the Spirit's Guidance	29
	3		3:13-17	The Servant's Baptism	30
			4:1-11	Deliverance from Temptation	31
	3		4:12-25	The Christian Mission	32
	2		5:1-12	Abundant Blessings	33
	2		5:13-16	Salt of the Earth, Light of the World	34
1			5:17-19	Fulfilling the Law and the Prophets	35
		4	5:20-26	Reconciling with One Another	36
			5:27-32	Grace-Filled Marriage	37
			5:33-37	Practicing Personal Integrity	38
	2		5:38-42	Forgiveness Rather Than Retaliation	39
	2		5:43-48	Love for Enemies	40
	2		6:1-6, 16-18	The Motives of Charity	41
			6:7-15	Prayer of the Heart	42
			6:19-23	Treasures in Heaven	43
	2		6:24-34	Serve God and Worry Not	44
			7:1-6	Freedom from the Tyranny of Judging Others	45
	2		7:7-12	Prayer According to God's Will	46
			7:13-20	Bearing Good Fruit for the Kingdom	47
	2		7:21-29	Acting upon the Father's Will	48
			8:1-4	Jesus' Healing Works	49
			8:5-13	The Authority of Jesus	50
			8:14-17	The Fullness of Jesus' Healing	51
			8:18-22	The Costs of Discipleship	52
			8:23-27	Faith in Times of Crisis	53
			8:28-34	Allowing Jesus to Heal Us	54
			9:1-8	Signs of the Kingdom	55
			9:9-13	Responding to Jesus' Call	56
			9:14-17	Christ Brings Renewal	57
			9:18-26	Toward a Deeper Faith	58

Plan	Passage	Theme	Page
	9:27-31	Faith as Intelligent Adherence	59
	9:32-38	Jesus, the Compassionate Shepherd	60
1	10:1-7	Commissioning the Apostles to Preach	61
	10:8-15	Reliance on God	62
	10:16-23	Guidance for Coming Persecution	63
	10:24-33	Comfort and Strength in Christ	64
	10:34–11:1	Taking Up the Cross	65
	11:2-15	He Who Is to Come	66
	11:16-19	Wisdom Justified by Deeds	67
	11:20-24	Accepting Our Hope for Salvation	68
	11:25-27	A Childlike Openness to God	69
	11:28-30	Peace in the Life of Christ	70
4	12:1-8	The Primacy of Mercy	71
	12:9-13	Righteousness by Faith	72
3	12:14-21	Recognizing the Messiah	73
	12:22-37	Destroying Satan's Reign	74
	12:38-42	The Sign of the Cross	75
	12:43-45	Shutting Out Evil	76
	12:46-50	God's Spiritual Family	77
1	13:1-9	Rooted in Good Soil	78
	13:10-17	Accepting the Message with Open Hearts	79
4	13:18-23	Yielding Plentiful Fruit	80
	13:24-30	Awaiting the Harvest	81
	13:31-35	Growth Comes from God	82
	13:36-43	Leaving Judgment to Christ	83
	13:44-46	The Kingdom Treasure	84
	13:47-52	Treasures, Old and New	85
	13:53-58	Seeing All Things Anew	86
	14:1-12	The Courage to Follow Christ	87
	14:13-21	The Abundance of Grace	88
4	14:22-36	Trusting in the Lord	89
	15:1-20	Wholehearted Devotion to God	90
	15:21-28	Blessings Available to All	91
	15:29-39	Miracles—Past, Present, and Future	92
	16:1-12	Asking for Signs	93
3	16:13-20	The Christ, the Son of the Living God	94
	16:21-28	The Difficult Wisdom of the Cross	95
3	17:1-9	Transformed into the Image of Christ	96

Plan	Passage	Theme	Page
	17:10-13	Recognizing the Messiah	97
	17:14-21	Faith as a Grain of Mustard Seed	98
	17:22-27	The Son of Man Who Reigns	99
	18:1-11	Developing a Spirit of Humility	100
	18:12-14	The Shepherd Seeks Lost Sheep	101
	18:15-20	Reproving One Another in Love	102
4	18:21-35	Forgiveness from the Heart, Without Limit	103
	19:1-12	Upholding the Sanctity of Marriage	104
	19:13-15	Leading Children to Christ	105
	19:16-22	God, Our First Priority	106
	19:23-30	God's Rightful Place	107
1	20:1-16	The Privilege of Serving Christ	108
	20:17-28	The Cup of Service	109
	20:29-34	The Earnest Cry of Faith	110
3	21:1-11	Jesus' Humble Entry into Jerusalem	111
	21:12-17	Offering Pleasing Sacrifices to God	112
	21:18-22	Nurturing a Fruitful Faith	113
	21:23-27	Authority from the Heavenly Father	114
	21:28-32	Responding to God's Will	115
	21:33-46	Living in and for Christ	116
	22:1-14	Many Are Called, but Few Are Chosen	117
	22:15-22	Performing Christian Political Service	118
	22:23-33	The Living Hope of Resurrection	119
	22:34-40	The Law of Love	120
	22:41-46	The Lordship of the Son of David	121
	23:1-12	Abandoning Self to Serve Others	122
	23:13-36	The Woes of Injustice and Unrighteousness	123
	23:37-39	Crucifixion: The Road of Salvation	124
3	24:1-35	The Coming Day of the Lord	125
	24:36-44	Preparing Our Hearts for Union with God	126
	24:45-51	The Vigilance of the Faithful Servant	127
4	25:1-13	The Readiness of the Wise	128
	25:14-30	Investing in Spiritual Prosperity	129
1	25:31-46	God's Blessings on the Sheepfold	130
1	26:1–27:66	The Passion of Christ	131
1	28:1-15	Kingdom Courage Overcomes Fear and Death	136
4	28:16-20	The Great Commission	137

APPENDIX 2

Reading through the Liturgical Year

The glossary of the *Catechism of the Catholic Church* defines the liturgical year as the celebration of "the mysteries of the Lord's birth, life, death, and resurrection in such a way that the entire year becomes a 'year of the Lord's grace.' Thus the cycle of the liturgical year and the great feasts constitute the basic rhythm of the Christian's life of prayer, with its focal point at Easter." We have included the following table as an invitation to you to join in this life of prayer and as a possible Bible reading and study plan. This table includes only the Sunday readings and feast day readings that you would also hear read during the indicated day's Mass. A daily listing of lectionary readings can be found at the United States Conference of Catholic Bishops Web site: www.usccb.org.

Cycle A	Cycle B	Cycle C
First Sunday of Advent		
Isaiah 2:1-5 Romans 13:11-14 Matthew 24:37-44	Isaiah 63:16-17, 19; 64:2-7 (NRSV: Isaiah 63:16-17, 19; 64:3-8) 1 Corinthians 1:3-9 Mark 13:33-37	Jeremiah 33:14-161 1 Thessalonians 3:12—4:2 Luke 21:25-28, 34-36
Second Sunday of Advent		
Isaiah 11:1-10 Romans 15:4-9 Matthew 3:1-12	Isaiah 40:1-5, 9-11 2 Peter 3:8-14 Mark 1:1-8	Baruch 5:1-9 Philippians 1:4-6, 8-11 Luke 3:1-6
Third Sunday of Advent		
Isaiah 35:1-6, 10 James 5:7-10 Matthew 11:2-11	Isaiah 61:1-2, 10-11 1 Thessalonians 5:16-24 John 1:6-8, 19-28	Zephaniah 3:14-18 Philippians 4:4-7 Luke 3:10-18
Fourth Sunday of Advent		
Isaiah 7:10-14 Romans 1:1-7 Matthew 1:18-24	2 Samuel 7:1-5, 8-12, 14, 16 Romans 16:25-27 Luke 1:26-38	Mic 5:1-4 Hebrews 10:5-10 Luke 1:39-45
Christmas (Midnight Mass)		
Isaiah 9:1-6 (NRSV: Isaiah 9:2-7) Titus 2:11-14 Luke 2:1-14	Isaiah 9:1-6 (NRSV: Isaiah 9:2-7) Titus 2:11-14 Luke 2:1-14	Isaiah 9:1-6 (NRSV: Isaiah 9:2-7) Titus 2:11-14 Luke 2:1-14
Christmas (Daytime Mass)		
Isaiah 52:7-10 Hebrews 1:1-6 John 1:1-18	Isaiah 52:7-10 Hebrews 1:1-6 John 1:1-18	Isaiah 52:7-10 Hebrews 1:1-6 John 1:1-18

Feast of the Holy Family		
Sirach 3:2-7, 12-14 Colossians 3:12-21 Matthew 2:13-15, 19-23	Sirach 3:2-7, 12-14 or Genesis 15:1-6; 21:1-3 Colossians 3:12-21 or Hebrews 11:8, 11-12, 17-19 Luke 2:22-40 or 22:39-40	Sirach 3:2-7, 12-14 or 1 Samuel 1:20-22, 24-28 Colossians 3:12-21 or 1 John 3:1-2, 21-24 Luke 2:41-52
Solemnity of Mary, Mother of God (January 1)		
Numbers 6:22-27 Galatians 4:4-7 Luke 2:16-21	Numbers 6:22-27 Galatians 4:4-7 Luke 2:16-21	Numbers 6:22-27 Galatians 4:4-7 Luke 2:16-21
Epiphany		
Isaiah 60:1-6 Ephesians 3:2-3, 5-6 Matthew 2:1-12	Isaiah 60:1-6 Ephesians 3:2-3, 5-6 Matthew 2:1-12	Isaiah 60:1-6 Ephesians 3:2-3, 5-6 Matthew 2:1-12
Baptism of the Lord		
Isaiah 42:1-4, 6-7 Acts 10:34-38 Matthew 3:13-17	Isaiah 42:1-4, 6-7 or Isaiah 55:1-11 Acts 10:34-38 or 1 John 5:1-9 Mark 1:7-11	Isaiah 42:1-4, 6-7 or Isaiah 40:1-5, 9-11 Acts 10:34-38 or Titus 2:11-14; 3:4-7 Luke 3:15-16, 21-22
Ash Wednesday		
Joel 2:12-18 2 Corinthians 5:20—6:2 Matthew 6:1-6, 16-18	Joel 2:12-18 2 Corinthians 5:20—6:2 Matthew 6:1-6, 16-18	Joel 2:12-18 2 Corinthians 5:20—6:2 Matthew 6:1-6, 16-18
First Sunday of Lent		
Genesis 2:7-9; 3:1-7 Romans 5:12-19 Matthew 4:1-11	Genesis 9:8-15 1 Peter 3:18-22 Mark 1:12-15	Deuteronomy 26:4-10 Romans 10:8-13 Luke 4:1-13
Second Sunday of Lent		
Genesis 12:1-4 2 Timothy 1:8-10 Matthew 17:1-9	Genesis 22:1-2, 9, 10-13, 15-18 Romans 8:31-34 Mark 9:2-10	Genesis 15:5-12, 17-18 Philippians 3:17—4:1 Luke 9:28-36
Third Sunday of Lent		
Exodus 17:3-7 Romans 5:1-2, 5-8 John 4:5-42	Exodus 20:1-17 1 Corinthians 1:22-25 John 2:13-25	Exodus 3:1-8, 13-15 1 Corinthians 10:1-6, 10-12 Luke 13:1-9
Fourth Sunday of Lent		
1 Samuel 16:1, 6-7, 10-13 Ephesians 5:8-14 John 9:1-41	2 Chronicles 36:14-16, 19-23 Ephesians 2:4-10 John 3:14-21	Joshua 5:9, 10-12 2 Corinthians 5:17-21 Luke 15:1-3, 11-32

Fifth Sunday of Lent		
Ezekiel 37:12-14 Romans 8:8-11 John 11:1-45	Jeremiah 31:31-34 Hebrews 5:7-9 John 12:20-33	Isaiah 43:16-21 Philippians 3:8-14 John 8:1-11
Passion Sunday (Palm Sunday)		
Isaiah 50:4-7 Philippians 2:6-11 Matthew 26:14—27:66	Isaiah 50:4-7 Philippians 2:6-11 Mark 14:1—15:47	Isaiah 50:4-7 Philippians 2:6-11 Luke 22:14—23:56
Mass of the Lord's Supper		
Exodus 12:1-8, 11-14 1 Corinthians 11:23-26 John 13:1-15	Exodus 12:1-8, 11-14 1 Corinthians 11:23-26 John 13:1-15	Exodus 12:1-8, 11-14 1 Corinthians 11:23-26 John 13:1-15
Good Friday		
Isaiah 52:13—53:12 Hebrews 4:14-16; 5:7-9 John 18:1—19:42	Isaiah 52:13—53:12 Hebrews 4:14-16; 5:7-9 John 18:1—19:42	Isaiah 52:13—53:12 Hebrews 4:14-16; 5:7-9 John 18:1—19:42
Easter Vigil		
Genesis 1:1—2:2 Genesis 22:1-18 Exodus 14:15—15:1 Isaiah 54:5-14 Isaiah 55:1-11 Baruch 3:9-15, 32—4:4 Ezekiel 36:16-17, 18-28 Romans 6:3-11 Matthew 28:1-10	Genesis 1:1—2:2 Genesis 22:1-18 Exodus 14:15—15:1 Isaiah 54:5-14 Isaiah 55:1-11 Baruch 3:9-15, 32—4:4 Ezekiel 36:16-17, 18-28 Romans 6:3-11 Mark 16:1-7	Genesis 1:1—2:2 Genesis 22:1-18 Exodus 14:15—15:1 Isaiah 54:5-14 Isaiah 55:1-11 Baruch 3:9-15, 32—4:4 Ezekiel 36:16-17, 18-28 Romans 6:3-11 Luke 24:1-12
Easter Sunday		
Acts 10:34, 37-43 Colossians 3:1-4 or 1 Corinthians 5:6-8 John 20:1-9	Acts 10:34, 37-43 Colossians 3:1-4 or 1 Corinthians 5:6-8 John 20:1-9	Acts 10:34, 37-43 Colossians 3:1-4 or 1 Corinthians 5:6-8 John 20:1-9
Second Sunday of Easter		
Acts 2:42-47 1 Peter 1:3-9 John 20:19-31	Acts 4:32-35 1 John 5:1-6 John 20:19-31	Acts 5:12-16 Revelation 1:9-11, 12-13, 17-19 John 20:19-31
Third Sunday of Easter		
Acts 2:14, 22-33 1 Peter 1:17-21 Luke 24:13-35	Acts 3:13-15, 17-19 1 John 2:1-5 Luke 24:35-48	Acts 5:27-32, 40-41 Revelation 5:11-14 John 21:1-19 or John 21:1-14
Fourth Sunday of Easter		
Acts 2:14, 36-41 1 Peter 2:20-25 John 10:1-10	Acts 4:8-12 1 John 3:1-2 John 10:11-18	Acts 13:14, 43-52 Revelation 7:9, 14-17 John 10:27-30

Fifth Sunday of Easter		
Acts 6:1-7 1 Peter 2:4-9 John 14:1-12	Acts 9:26-31 1 John 3:18-24 John 15:1-8	Acts 14:21-27 Revelation 21:1-5 John 13:31-35
Sixth Sunday of Easter		
Acts 8:5-8, 14-17 1 Peter 3:15-18 John 14:15-21	Acts 10:25-26, 34-35, 44-48 1 John 4:7-10 John 15:9-17	Acts 15:1-2, 22-29 Revelation 21:10-14, 22-23 John 14:23-29
Ascension of Our Lord		
Acts 1:1-11 Ephesians 1:17-23 Matthew 28:16:20	Acts 1:1-11 Ephesians 1:17-23 or Ephesians 4:1-13 Mark 16:15-20	Acts 1:1-11 Ephesians 1:17-23 or Hebrews 9:24-28; 10:19-23 Luke 24:46-53
Seventh Sunday of Easter		
Acts 1:12-14 1 Peter 4:13-16 John 17:1-11	Acts 1:15-17, 20-26 1 John 4:11-16 John 17:11-19	Acts 7:55-60 Revelation 22:12-14, 16-17, 20 John 17:20-26
Pentecost Sunday		
Acts 2:1-11 1 Corinthians 12:3-7, 12-13 John 20:19-23	Acts 2:1-11 1 Corinthians 12:3-7, 12-13 or Galatians 5:16-25 John 20:19-23 or John 15:26-27; 16:12-15	Acts 2:1-11 1 Corinthians 12:3-7, 12-13 or Romans 8:8-17 John 20:19-23 or John 14:15-16, 23-26
First Sunday in Ordinary Time		
(See Baptism of the Lord, above)	(See Baptism of the Lord, above)	(See Baptism of the Lord, above)
Second Sunday in Ordinary Time		
Isaiah 49:3, 5-6 1 Corinthians 1:1-3 John 1:29-34	1 Samuel 3:3-10, 19 1 Corinthians 6:13-15, 17-20 John 1:35-42	Isaiah 62:1-5 1 Corinthians 12:4-11 John 2:1-11
Third Sunday in Ordinary Time		
Isaiah 8:23—9:3 1 Corinthians 1:10-13, 17 Matthew 4:12-23	Jonah 3:1-5, 10 1 Corinthians 7:29-31 Mark 1:14-20	Nehemiah 8:2-4, 5-6, 8-10 1 Corinthians 12:12-30 Luke 1:1-4; 4:14-21
Fourth Sunday in Ordinary Time		
Zephaniah 2:3; 3:12-13 1 Corinthians 1:26-31 Matthew 5:1-12	Deuteronomy 18:15-20 1 Corinthians 7:32-35 Mark 1:21-28	Jeremiah 1:4-5, 17-19 1 Corinthians 12:31—13:13 Luke 4:21-30
Fifth Sunday in Ordinary Time		
Isaiah 58:7-10 1 Corinthians 2:1-5 Matthew 5:13-16	Job 7:1-4, 6-7 1 Corinthians 9:16-19, 22-23 Mark 1:29-39	Isaiah 6:1-2, 3-8 1 Corinthians 15:1-11 Luke 5:1-11

Sixth Sunday in Ordinary Time		
Sirach 15:15-20 1 Corinthians 2:6-10 Matthew 5:17-37	Leviticus 13:1-2, 44-46 1 Corinthians 10:31—11:1 Mark 1:40-45	Jeremiah 17:5-8 1 Corinthians 15:12, 16-20 Luke 6:17, 20-26
Seventh Sunday in Ordinary Time		
Leviticus 19:1-2, 17-18 1 Corinthians 3:16-23 Matthew 5:38-48	Isaiah 43:18-19, 21-22 2 Corinthians 1:18-22 Mark 2:1-12	1 Samuel 26:2, 7-9, 12-13, 22-23 1 Corinthians 15:45-49 Luke 6:27-38
Eighth Sunday in Ordinary Time		
Isaiah 49:14-15 1 Corinthians 4:1-5 Matthew 6:24-34	Hosea 2:16, 17, 21-22 2 Corinthians 3:1-6 Mark 2:18-22	Sirach 27:4-7 1 Corinthians 15:54-58 Luke 6:39-45
Ninth Sunday in Ordinary Time		
Deuteronomy 11:18, 26-28, 32 Romans 3:21-25, 28 Matthew 7:21-27	Deuteronomy 5:12-15 2 Corinthians 4:6-11 Mark 2:23—3:6	1 Kings 8:41-43 Galatians 1:1-2, 6-10 Luke 7:1-10
Tenth Sunday in Ordinary Time		
Hosea 6:3-6 Romans 4:18-25 Matthew 9:9-13	Genesis 3:9-15 2 Corinthians 4:13—5:1 Mark 3:20-35	1 Kings 17:17-24 Galatians 1:11-19 Luke 7:11-17
Eleventh Sunday in Ordinary Time		
Exodus 19:2-6 Romans 5:6-11 Matthew 9:36—10:8	Ezekiel 17:22-24 2 Corinthians 5:6-10 Mark 4:26-34	2 Samuel 12:7-10, 13 Galatians 2:16, 19-21 Luke 7:36—8:3
Twelfth Sunday in Ordinary Time		
Jeremiah 20:10-13 Romans 5:12-15 Matthew 10:26-33	Job 38:1, 8-11 2 Corinthians 5:14-17 Mark 4:35-41	Zechariah 12:10-11 Galatians 3:26-29 Luke 9:18-24
Thirteenth Sunday in Ordinary Time		
2 Kings 4:8-11, 14-16 Romans 6:3-4, 8-11 Matthew 10:37-42	Wisdom 1:13-15; 2:23-24 2 Corinthians 8:7, 9, 13-15 Mark 5:21-43	1 Kings 19:16, 19-21 Galatians 5:1, 13-18 Luke 9:51-62
Fourteenth Sunday in Ordinary Time		
Zechariah 9:9-10 Romans 8:9, 11-13 Matthew 11:25-30	Ezekiel 2:2-5 2 Corinthians 12:7-10 Mark 6:1-6	Isaiah 66:10-14 Galatians 6:14-18 Luke 10:1-12, 17-20
Fifteenth Sunday in Ordinary Time		
Isaiah 55:10-11 Romans 8:18-23 Matthew 13:1-23	Amos 7:12-15 Ephesians 1:3-14 Mark 6:7-13	Deuteronomy 30:10-14 Colossians 1:15-20 Luke 10:25-37

Sixteenth Sunday in Ordinary Time		
Wisdom 12:13, 16-19 Romans 8:26-27 Matthew 13:24-43	Jeremiah 23:1-6 Ephesians 2:13-18 Mark 6:30-34	Genesis 18:1-10 Colossians 1:24-28 Luke 10:38-42
Seventeenth Sunday in Ordinary Time		
1 Kings 3:5, 7-12 Romans 8:28-30 Matthew 13:44-52	2 Kings 4:42-44 Ephesians 4:1-6 John 6:1-15	Genesis 18:20-32 Colossians 2:12-14 Luke 11:1-13
Eighteenth Sunday in Ordinary Time		
Isaiah 55:1-3 Romans 8:35, 37-39 Matthew 14:13-21	Exodus 16:2-4, 12-15 Ephesians 4:17, 20-24 John 6:24-35	Ecclesiastes 1:2; 2:21-23 Colossians 3:1-5, 9-11 Luke 12:13-21
Nineteenth Sunday in Ordinary Time		
1 Kings 19:9, 11-13 Romans 9:1-5 Matthew 14:22-33	1 Kings 19:4-8 Ephesians 4:30—5:2 John 6:41-51	Wisdom 18:6-9 Hebrews 11:1-2, 8-19 Luke 12:32-48
Twentieth Sunday in Ordinary Time		
Isaiah 56:1, 6-7 Romans 11:13-15, 29-32 Matthew 15:21-28	Proverbs 9:1-6 Ephesians 5:15-20 John 6:51-58	Jeremiah 38:4-6, 8-10 Hebrews 12:1-4 Luke 12:49-53
Twenty-first Sunday in Ordinary Time		
Isaiah 22:19-23 Romans 11:33-36 Matthew 16:13-20	Joshua 24:1-2, 15-17, 18 Ephesians 5:21-32 John 6:60-69	Isaiah 66:18-21 Hebrews 12:5-7, 11-13 Luke 13:22-30
Twenty-second Sunday in Ordinary Time		
Jeremiah 20:7-9 Romans 12:1-2 Matthew 16:21-27	Deuteronomy 4:1-2, 6-8 James 1:17-18, 21-22, 27 Mark 7:1-8, 14-15, 21-23	Sirach 3:17-18, 20, 28-29 Hebrews 12:18-19, 22-24 Luke 14:1, 7-14
Twenty-third Sunday in Ordinary Time		
Ezekiel 33:7-9 Romans 13:8-10 Matthew 18:15-20	Isaiah 35:4-7 James 2:1-5 Mark 7:31-37	Wisdom 9:13-18 Philemon 9-10, 12-17 Luke 14:25-33
Twenty-fourth Sunday in Ordinary Time		
Sirach 27:30—28:7 Romans 14:7-9 Matthew 18:21-35	Isaiah 50:5-9 James 2:14-18 Mark 8:27-35	Exodus 32:7-11, 13-14 1 Timothy 1:12-17 Luke 15:1-32
Twenty-fifth Sunday in Ordinary Time		
Isaiah 55:6-9 Philippians 1:20-24, 27 Matthew 20:1-16	Wisdom 2:12, 17-20 James 3:16—4:3 Mark 9:30-37	Amos 8:4-7 1 Timothy 2:1-8 Luke 16:1-13

Twenty-sixth Sunday in Ordinary Time		
Ezekiel 18:25-28 Philippians 2:1-11 Matthew 21:28-32	Numbers 11:25-29 James 5:1-6 Mark 9:38-43, 45, 47-48	Amos 6:1, 4-7 1 Timothy 6:11-16 Luke 16:19-31
Twenty-seventh Sunday in Ordinary Time		
Isaiah 5:1-7 Philippians 4:6-9 Matthew 21:33-43	Genesis 2:18-24 Hebrews 2:9-11 Mark 10:2-16	Habakkuk 1:2-3; 2:2-4 2 Timothy 1:6-8, 13-14 Luke 17:5-10
Twenty-eighth Sunday in Ordinary Time		
Isaiah 25:6-10 Philippians 4:12-14, 19-20 Matthew 22:1-14	Wisdom 7:7-11 Hebrews 4:12-13 Mark 10:17-30	2 Kings 5:14-17 2 Timothy 2:8-13 Luke 17:11-19
Twenty-ninth Sunday in Ordinary Time		
Isaiah 45:1, 4-6 1 Thessalonians 1:1-5 Matthew 22:15-21	Isaiah 53:10-11 Hebrews 4:14-16 Mark 10:35-45	Exodus 17:8-13 2 Timothy 3:14—4:2 Luke 18:1-8
Thirtieth Sunday in Ordinary Time		
Exodus 22:20-26 1 Thessalonians 1:5-10 Matthew 22:34-40	Jeremiah 31:7-9 Hebrews 5:1-6 Mark 10:46-52	Sirach 35:12-14, 16-18 2 Timothy 4:6-8, 16-18 Luke 18:9-14
Thirty-first Sunday in Ordinary Time		
Malachi 1:14—2:2, 8-10 1 Thessalonians 2:7-9, 13 Matthew 23:1-12	Deuteronomy 6:2-6 Hebrews 7:23-28 Mark 12:28-34	Wisdom 11:22—12:2 2 Thessalonians 1:11—2:2 Luke 19:1-10
Thirty-second Sunday in Ordinary Time		
Wisdom 6:12-16 1 Thessalonians 4:13-18 Matthew 25:1-13	1 Kings 17:10-16 Hebrews 9:24-28 Mark 12:38-44	2 Maccabees 7:1-2, 9-14 2 Thessalonians 2:16—3:5 Luke 20:27-38
Thirty-third Sunday in Ordinary Time		
Proverbs 31:10-13, 19-20, 30-31 1 Thessalonians 5:1-6 Matthew 25:14-30	Daniel 12:1-3 Hebrews 10:11-14, 18 Mark 13:24-32	Malachi 3:19-20 2 Thessalonians 3:7-12 Luke 21:5-19
Thirty-fourth Sunday in Ordinary Time (Solemnity of Our Lord Jesus Christ the King)		
Ezekiel 34:11-12, 15-17 1 Corinthians 15:20-26, 28 Matthew 25:31-46	Daniel 7:13-14 Revelation 1:5-8 John 18:33-37	2 Samuel 5:1-3 Colossians 1:12-20 Luke 23:35-43

Notes

Notes

Notes

Notes